LOVE
LIKE
JESUS

The Beatitudes: A Pathway
to Spiritual Maturity

ROBERT L. MORRIS, JR.

WESTBOW
PRESS®
A DIVISION OF THOMAS NELSON
& ZONDERVAN

WestBow Press books may be ordered through booksellers or by contacting:

WestBow Press
A Division of Thomas Nelson & Zondervan
1663 Liberty Drive
Bloomington, IN 47403
www.westbowpress.com
844-714-3454

Because of the dynamic nature of the Internet, any web addresses or
links contained in this book may have changed since publication and
may no longer be valid. The views expressed in this work are solely those
of the author and do not necessarily reflect the views of the publisher,
and the publisher hereby disclaims any responsibility for them.

Any people depicted in stock imagery provided by Getty Images are
models, and such images are being used for illustrative purposes only.
Certain stock imagery © Getty Images.

Scripture quotations are from New Revised Standard Version Bible,
copyright © 1989 National Council of the Churches of Christ in the United
States of America. Used by permission. All rights reserved worldwide.

ISBN: 978-1-6642-5811-2 (sc)
ISBN: 978-1-6642-5812-9 (hc)
ISBN: 978-1-6642-5810-5 (e)

Library of Congress Control Number: 2022903213

Print information available on the last page.

WestBow Press rev. date: 04/04/2022

This book is dedicated to the members and staff of First Presbyterian Church in Jacksonville, Florida. Special recognition goes to Brenda Baker, who served seventeen years as the clerk of the session (and often was my brain) without once seeking the spotlight or accolades. These dear friends and colleagues loved Jesus, worked, served, laughed, cried, and sacrificed. To the elders, deacons, trustees, staff, teachers, volunteers, prayer warriors, and congregants: serving alongside you was an honor. Our reward wasn't a church with thousands in attendance. Our reward was better; we got to see more of Jesus.

CONTENTS

CHAPTER 1

THE ANSWER IS LOVE

I HAD BEEN SERVING as the senior minister at First Presbyterian Church in Jacksonville for almost two years. It was not an easy ministry, as if any are. Urban blight, sprawling suburbs, and racial tensions were all elements in a recipe making much of downtown an urban desert. Some came downtown to work, while most never came to the city center unless there was a concert at the city's coliseum or attending a sporting event in the football stadium. For most people, the urban core was a place to be avoided.

There was a time when more than a dozen vibrant churches from varying denominations served this neighborhood. What remained was just a handful. The ones that survived were declining—some more than others. At my church, the sanctuary steps were occupied by the homeless during the day and our bushes became their home by night.

At one time, First Presbyterian Church (FPC) had been a thriving church in what was once a highly desired neighborhood. That was now ancient history. Houses were bulldozed to make way for commercial buildings. The few homes that remained were now lawyers' and bail bond offices or flophouses.

The church campus included three old but stately buildings and a gas station that backed up to the education building. Decades ago, these were pristine and spectacular edifices dedicated to Christ and His work. But over the years, declining membership meant declining income, which meant deferred maintenance.

When the Lord called us to serve FPC, we discovered every roof leaked, plaster was falling off some walls, bathrooms were outdated, and everything needed painting. The sanctuary's PA system worked most of the time, and our organist played the keys on the hundred-year-old pipe organ that still worked (avoiding the keys that were now lifeless).

One weekday morning, I arrived at the church before 8 a.m. and found shards of glass in the parking lot. At first, I assumed someone had shattered beer bottles on the gravel parking lot. But then I noticed wood fragments mixed in with the glass. I looked up and saw that an entire window was missing from the church education building. Overnight, it had just fallen out of the building. It was a blessing that it happened when it did, so no one was hurt. The place needed work, and each day, a new need raised its hand and demanded attention.

Before my arrival, there was some debate about whether the church should close or move to the suburbs. When the vote was taken, the church chose to remain a city church, but many who voted to leave did just that; they moved on. It was understandable why so many left. We had little income, massive campus repairs looming, and few programs. It was a dire situation.

About seventy people were in attendance on my first Sunday, and they welcomed me with cautious enthusiasm. We all worked hard and jumped in with both feet, and God honored our efforts. After almost two years, we had grown some (in attendance), and the church culture began to change. We were more than a religious agency serving the poor; we were becoming a vital church. We still served those in need, but now Christ was first and foremost in everything we said and did. Interest in the Bible had ignited. I am grateful to this day for those who worked so hard to help rebuild the spiritual life of the grand old church.

We had worked, prayed, laughed, and cried. We were together, and we were a team. After a couple of years, the church was off what I called "spiritual life support." We could pay our bills and even hire some staff. But what now? Where did we go from here? We still were small in numbers, with a church in a desolate part of the city. There were lots of fine churches in the suburbs that were closer to Jacksonville's population centers. These suburban churches had more staff, more money, and more programs, and their facilities were clean and modern (at least compared to ours). Why would anyone drive downtown to a church when so many thriving churches were close to their homes?

I began to pray and ask the Lord how to move the church forward. Did we need a great associate minister or a children's director? Or maybe some program that no one else had like a Christian drama ministry? Or some sort of youth soccer league? Weeks went by. I prayed, read books on the topic, called clergy friends, and bounced ideas off them. One day, Jesus showed me what our next step would be.

It happened in early December when, one chilly morning, my office phone rang. The caller was a Hispanic mom in crisis. She was so desperate, and she was calling random churches asking for help. Somehow, she found our church's phone number online. Her family had been evicted from their small apartment. Maintenance men from the complex stacked her family's furniture and clothing on the street curb, where scavengers hauled it off. She had many children and little money, and she was scared.

She got enough money to rent another apartment but had no food, furniture, or clothing. We found out how many beds she needed and the clothing sizes of her kids. We shared the need with the church, and donations poured in the very next Sunday. The following day, we organized volunteers to deliver the items to the family. Virginia, my wife, drove our SUV to the church, and we began to load up some bedding.

Virginia and I were carrying a mattress to our vehicle (I

was walking backward) when a woman I had never seen before asked me if I was the pastor. I continued hauling the bedding, and I told her I was. Then she asked if I could help her. As we loaded the SUV, she told me she needed a bus ticket to her home someplace out of town. I told her I would help her if she would help us load the vehicle. She cheerfully jumped in. As we hauled boxes to the Trailblazer, I remember thinking that this woman was different from other people who had come to the church looking for help. I never got her name, but there was something elegant about her. She dressed like a business executive, and her long winter coat looked very expensive. She was an older African American woman and had the vocabulary of a college professor. She had a charming smile and not a visible wrinkle on her face.

The bus station was just a few short blocks away, and I told her I would meet her there and buy her a bus ticket to get home for Christmas. Virginia drove me and waited in the packed SUV as I entered the Greyhound station. We had learned from past mistakes to never give people money or buy a bus ticket in the rider's name; they often would resell it or try to get a refund to get the cash. So each time we purchased a bus ticket for someone, a church staff person had to accompany the traveler and buy the ticket in the church's name. This day it was my turn.

When I entered the Greyhound station, I was surprised that only four of us were in the station: a security guard, a ticket agent, the woman we were trying to help, and me. I asked the polite traveler to follow me to the ticket window, where we could make the purchase. At the window, I told the agent we needed a one-way ticket for this woman and that it would be purchased in the church's name. She asked us to wait as she went into another room to collect some forms we would need to fill out. While we waited, the kindly traveler, who was standing a little behind me, said to me, "Your Father in heaven wants you to know He is proud of you." I thanked her for her kind words, but in truth, I thought it was her way of saying thanks for helping her.

When the ticket agent returned, the agent asked me for the passenger's name and destination. I turned to ask the woman to provide that information, and she was gone. I mean, really gone. At first, I thought she had wandered off. So I looked all over the station, which was not very large, but she was nowhere to be found. I asked the security guard posted by the bathroom entrances if a well-dressed woman had gone into the ladies' room. He told me no one had been in there for a long while. I went outside, walked around the building—nothing.

Finally, I got back in the SUV with my wife and told her about the peculiar disappearance. We were both bewildered but went on to deliver the furniture and clothing to the family in need.

Nothing like this had ever happened to me before. I shared the story with a colleague, who asked, "Could she have been an angel delivering a message?" I had no idea. I had never met an angel. Or was she just a kind homeless woman who said something nice? There is no way of knowing. I do know this:

whoever this woman was, she shared some words that have stuck with me to this day.

My Heavenly Father was pleased that our church helped that Hispanic mom and her children and tried to help an older woman get home for Christmas. Serving those in need is the loudest sermon on love one can witness. This event, and others like it, revealed the direction the church should go.

Jesus made me see that we didn't need more money or staff or new buildings to love as Jesus loved. My years of ministry experience taught me that people wanted to participate with our Lord to help change lives. People don't come to church just to warm a pew or hear a snappy sermon. People wanted to belong to a church where lives are changed, and there is authentic love in action. So if visitors experienced that when they worshipped with us, many would join us.

This book is the story of how I (and others in the church) learned to love more and more like Jesus. Did we make mistakes? Of course, I (we) made many mistakes. And I wish I had some do-overs. But God uses our successes and failures to shape us spiritually. Learning to love like Jesus was and continues to be a process carried out within us by the Holy Spirit. In our particular journey, we learned some lessons and truths that changed me, my leadership style, and many at FPC. But it didn't happen overnight.

※

CHAPTER 2

GOD LOVES US TOO MUCH TO LEAVE US THE WAY WE ARE

WHEN PARENTS HAVE their first child, it is an awe-filled experience. That infant becomes the center of the parents' world. That baby controls when parents sleep and how they spend their money and even becomes the focus of most conversations. Pictures are snapped, and videos are shared with friends and family. Parents love their children in ways that are both instinctual and divine. Parenting is an exhaustive and often trying experience to be cherished.

But as much as parents love their infants, no parent wants their child to stay an infant. I would go even further and say that God designed parenting in such a way that when parents are so tired of whatever stage their child is in, just when the parents are about to pull their hair out—it is at that moment the child begins to transition to the next stage of life. From infant to toddler, from toddler to three-year-old, from there to nursery school, and so on. The point is this: *parents love their kids just as they are but also want to see them grow and become all that God has designed them to be.*

That's the way God loves you and me. The Lord loves us and accepts us just like we are (that is called grace) but loves us too much to leave us that way. When we first become believers, Jesus welcomes us with a profound and unfathomable grace into his family. Of course, there has to be some sort of repentance in the believer's heart; there has to be a turning away from old sins. But truth be told, when we were new believers, none of us could grasp the depth of our sin and brokenness. For example, when I gave my life to Christ as a high school student, I repented of the sin I knew of in my life, unaware of the total depravity that is the human experience. So I repented of what I was aware of, and at that moment, Christ began a process of giving me a new heart. As I have traveled through life with Jesus as my Shepherd, He has continuously shown me places in my life that needed redemption. There are character traits, impure motives, and selfish desires that all need to be transformed by the Holy Spirit. That process is called sanctification, from the Latin word *sanctus,* which means "holy." Sanctification is what the Holy Spirit does in us to make us holy; the Spirit works within us to make us more and more like Jesus.

Like children, we all grow spiritually at different rates. For some, this process of growing into mature believers begins quickly. That's what happened to Zacchaeus (Luke 19:1–10[1]). The story of Zacchaeus opens with Jesus passing through Jericho. Zacchaeus, a tax collector, lived there and was well-known in his community, not because he was a stellar citizen but because he wasn't. To be sure, he was a traitor. Zacchaeus was a tax collector for the hated Romans, who occupied that part of the world. The Roman army was a ruthless and harsh occupier. Zacchaeus made himself wealthy by collecting taxes from fellow Jews and paid the Romans their share while keeping a percentage. In short, Zacchaeus got rich from the tax money he collected from his countrymen.

The text doesn't say how Zacchaeus knew of Jesus or how he knew Jesus was coming to town that day. However, he learned Jesus was passing through, and he was determined to at least see this man who claimed to be God. The crowds were large when Jesus arrived in Jericho, so much so Zacchaeus couldn't see Jesus through the crowd that filled the streets. So he ran ahead, climbed a sycamore tree, and waited for Jesus to pass by. Hardly a dignified thing to do by one of Jericho's wealthiest citizens.

Jesus came to the place where Zacchaeus had perched. Jesus looked up and said to him, "Zacchaeus, hurry and come down; for I must stay at your house today" (verse 5). Jesus going to Zacchaeus's home startled the crowd; after all, why would Jesus

---

[1] All scripture quoted is from the New Revised Standard Version of the Bible.

go to the home of a sinner and traitor? But Jesus did go despite the grumbling crowd. The Bible doesn't tell us everything that happened that day between Zacchaeus and Jesus, but one thing we do know is it changed Zacchaeus's life. In verse 8, Zacchaeus said to the Lord, "Look, half of my possessions, Lord, I will give to the poor; and if I have defrauded anyone of anything, I will pay back four times as much." Jesus says, "Today salvation has come to this house because he too is a son of Abraham. For the Son of Man came to seek out and to save the lost" (verses 9–10).

Zacchaeus was a changed man. His values, priorities, and heart were radically changed in one day after meeting the King of Kings. For some, being transformed by Jesus comes at Zacchaeus's speed, and it is evident to all who have eyes to see. But others struggle to grow.

Matthew's Gospel (chapter 19, starting with the sixteenth verse) tells of another of Jesus's encounters. In this meeting (we never learn his name), the text tells us he was young, religious, and wealthy. Yet this young man knew something was missing in his life, and he came to Jesus, hoping to find what his soul yearned for. The text says,

> Then someone came to him and said, "Teacher, what good deed must I do to have eternal life?" And he said to him, "Why do you ask me about what is good? There is only one who is good. If you wish to enter into life, keep the commandments."

He said to him, "Which ones?" And Jesus said, "You shall not murder; You shall not commit adultery; You shall not steal; You shall not bear false witness; Honor your father and mother; also, You shall love your neighbor as yourself." The young man said to him, "I have kept all these; what do I still lack?" Jesus said to him, "If you wish to be perfect, go, sell your possessions, and give the money to the poor, and you will have treasure in heaven; then come, follow me." When the young man heard this word, he went away grieving, for he had many possessions. Then Jesus said to his disciples, "Truly I tell you, it will be hard for a rich person to enter the kingdom of heaven. Again I tell you, it is easier for a camel to go through the eye of a needle than for someone who is rich to enter the kingdom of God." When the disciples heard this, they were greatly astounded and said, "Then who can be saved?" But Jesus looked at them and said, "For mortals it is impossible, but for God all things are possible."

This young man came to Jesus with a hunger in his heart that the things of the world and all his accomplishments could not satisfy. He was looking for more than religiosity; he was looking for something real, something that was bigger than himself. He had everything that the world uses to gauge success, but he knew something was missing. He was everything that Zacchaeus wasn't—respected, auspicious, and religious, but he was just as lost, and he knew it.

There are a lot of people in the world like that—people who seem to have everything the world can offer yet their hearts yearn for something more. If you have kids or grandkids, then you know who Fred Rogers was. You may not know him by that name, but every little kid and every parent who has a TV knows him by Mr. Rogers of the TV show *Mr. Rogers' Neighborhood*, which is on every morning on public television. Something else you might not have known about him is that Mr. Rogers was Presbyterian minister whose entire ministry was to children. But his ministry touched more than children. In 1997 he received a Lifetime Achievement Award at the Emmy Awards. Esquire[2] published an account of the memorable moment, writing,

> [Mister Rogers] went onstage to accept Emmy's Lifetime Achievement Award, and there, in front of all the soap-opera stars and talk-show sinceratrons, in front of all the jutting man-tanned jaws and jutting saltwater bosoms, he made his small bow and said into the microphone, "All of us have special ones who have loved us into being. Would you just take, along with me, ten seconds to think of the people who have helped you become who you are ... Ten seconds of

---

[2] http://mentalfloss.com/article/27237/mister-rogers-and-his-lifetime-achievement-emmy-get-ready-cry-work. The video is still available online.

silence." And then he lifted his wrist, and looked at the audience, and looked at his watch, and said softly, "I'll watch the time," and there was, at first, a small whoop from the crowd, a giddy, strangled hiccup of laughter, as people realized that he wasn't kidding, that Mister Rogers was not some convenient eunuch but rather a man, an authority figure who actually expected them to do what he asked ... and so they did. One second, two seconds, three seconds ... and now the jaws clenched, and the bosoms heaved, and the mascara ran, and the tears fell upon the beglittered gathering like rain leaking down a crystal chandelier, and Mister Rogers finally looked up from his watch and said, "May God be with you" to all his vanquished children.

We have all seen award shows with actors, singers, and celebrities recognized for their talents. Many of these recipients accepted their awards with arrogance, political statements, and even at times, self-aggrandizement. Mr. Rogers was different. Amid the Hollywood glitz, Fred Rogers asked the audience to stop thinking about themselves or their careers and for ten seconds to think about those people who had been there for them. Those ten seconds of authenticity brought tears to actors and actresses who, for a moment, stopped posturing and pretending to be something they weren't. Looking back on that event, Fred Rogers said, "I think we don't realize how hungry people are for what is honest and real."

Fred Rogers was right! We are all hungry for what is honest and genuine. So was this rich, young ruler. He wasn't just hungry; he was starving. Along with youth, health, and financial resources, he was also very religious. To be a good, moral Jewish person back then, that was no easy task. There were hundreds of rules to follow, and from the sound of the text, he was proud of the fact that he kept them with diligence. He had it all. Yet his soul cried out for more. He was looking for something that money, power, and being religious couldn't satisfy. His life was full but not satisfied. Aren't we all like that sometimes?

Have you ever come home from work or school in the late afternoon and are starving but not sure what you are hungry for? If you are like me, I first go to the refrigerator, open the door, and taste things. (My wife calls this "grazing.") I might try a grilled shrimp leftover from dinner the night before, or maybe a pickle, a slice of cheese, or a hard-boiled egg. Then I go to the pantry and eat a few Wheat Thins, a handful of peanuts, or a couple of potato chips. When I am hungry, I might take a bite of six to ten different food items, never finding the elusive taste I am yearning for, and then it hits me that I just ruined my dinner. And even worse, *I am now full but still not satisfied.*

That phrase, *full but not satisfied*, captures well the life of the rich, young ruler and many of us today. We all long for significance, meaning, and happiness. So the world tells us that the way we achieve happiness is by making money, and the more, the better. So we study hard in school and collect diplomas, and we get good jobs and welcome awards, promotions, and pay raises. We get married and start families. We take out mortgages and save for our kids' college. Then we wake up one day exhausted and glance at our calendars to find we are frantically busy but have spent little quality time with our spouses and kids. We look around and see we have accumulated a tremendous amount of stuff (primarily through credit card debt) that no one will want when we die, and we go to church occasionally but never really connect "to the God thing." We realize we are like the rich, young ruler: our lives are not just full but frantically busy, and we have spent our lives making bosses and customers happy, but deep down, we know we are an inch deep and a mile wide with those we love (especially God).

Notice that Jesus doesn't congratulate the young man on being successful, religious, or well respected. Jesus doesn't hand him a synagogue pledge card or ask him to join a vital church committee. Jesus is more concerned about the state of his soul than the state of his bank book. No, Jesus sees through the veneer of this man's shallow life and calls him to give away his money and follow Him. At that moment, the young ruler had to decide the direction of his life and his very soul. Would he abandon his worldly wealth and accomplishments to follow Jesus, or would he choose to continue to chase after the things that kept his life spiritually malnourished? The rich, young ruler came face-to-face with the One who could have given him what his soul longed for, yet he chose to cling to the things that bankrupted his soul.

These two people sought Jesus. Zacchaeus (the well-known sinner) repented and followed Jesus, and the rich, young ruler (respected, successful, and influential) turned away. Both men were lost and came to Jesus, knowing they needed something new in their lives. One received it; the other rejected Jesus's truth. But don't miss the point: Jesus knew they were lost, and He didn't allow either of them to stay where they were. Jesus moved them both forward in their spiritual journeys. Zacchaeus found his Savior; the rich, young ruler discovered how lost he still was. Both are essential steps in their faith journeys. For both, their stories don't end here. Scripture doesn't tell us what ultimately happens next in their lives. Will Zacchaeus remain faithful, or does he return to tax collecting? Will the rich, young ruler discover money will never satisfy a hungry heart and follow God?

We don't know how their stories end. But one thing we do know is Jesus is in the business of changing hearts. How is Jesus working in your life now? How is He sanctifying you? Read on. Jesus wants to teach us to love like Him.

CHAPTER 3

WHAT IS THIS LOVE?

EVERY FOUR YEARS, we hold presidential elections, and the process can be very confusing, especially for kids. Mike Wilson,[3] an elementary teacher in Ballwin, Missouri, asked his students to write some essays on the American political system. Here is what some of his students wrote:

- Calling a person a runner-up is a polite way of saying you lost.
- It is possible to get the majority of electoral votes without getting the majority of popular votes. Anyone who can ever understand how this works gets to be president.

[3] https://www.netfunny.com/rhf/jokes/88q2/29609.4.html, published 1984.

- The more I think about trying to run for president, the less I think of it.

- The president has the power to appoint and disappoint the members of his cabinet.

- In January, the president makes his inaugural address after he has been sworn at.

- The job of delegates is to resent their states.

- A dark horse is a candidate that the delegates don't know enough about to dislike yet.

- A split ticket is when you don't like any of them on the ticket, so you tear it up.

- When they talk about the most promising presidential candidate, they mean the one who can think of the most things to promise.

- Elephants and donkeys never fought until politics came along.

- Political strategy is when you don't let people know you have run out of ideas and keep shouting anyway.

- A candidate should always renounce his words carefully.

- We are learning how to make our election results known quicker and quicker. It is our campaigns we are having trouble getting any shorter.

- Campaigns give us a great deal of happiness by finally ending.

Trying to understand the American political system can be difficult at times, but we must understand it and participate in it to be responsible citizens. It is foundational to our gathered life.

When we think about following Jesus Christ, foundational things are there too. And most importantly, being a Christ follower means we are called to love others as Jesus loves us. Being loving people is a foundational part of our faith. Ephesians 3:16–17 says it like this:

> I pray that, according to the riches of his glory, may he grant that you may be strengthened in your inner being with power through his Spirit, and that Christ may dwell in your hearts through faith, as you are being rooted and grounded in love.

Jesus wants us to be rooted and grounded in love, which comes from following Jesus. Once our relationship with Christ is healthy, then He will teach us how to love our families and our neighbors, even the people we don't like. Jesus said it like this (Matthew 5:38–48):

> "You have heard that it was said, 'An eye for an eye and a tooth for a tooth.' But I say to you, do not resist an evildoer. But if anyone strikes you on the right cheek, turn the other also; and if anyone wants to sue you and take your coat, give your cloak as well; and if anyone forces you to go one mile, go also the second mile. Give to everyone who begs from you, and do not refuse anyone who wants to borrow from you.

"You have heard that it was said, 'You shall love your neighbor and hate your enemy.' But I say to you, love your enemies and pray for those who persecute you, so that you may be children of your Father in heaven; for he makes his sun rise on the evil and on the good, and sends rain on the righteous and on the unrighteous. For if you love those who love you, what reward do you have? Do not even the tax collectors do the same? And if you greet only your brothers and sisters, what more are you doing than others? Do not even the Gentiles do the same? Be perfect, therefore, as your heavenly Father is perfect.

This kind of love is radical and counterculture. Love, the way God wants us to love, is otherworldly, transforming, and redeeming. It is, in my view, the most powerful force on earth.

To understand this holy love, we need to define our words. In English, the word *love* means all kinds of things. For example, when we get married, we say we love our spouses, but we will also say we love pizza. Does that mean we care about our spouses the same way we like pizza? Of course not. We use the term *love* in our culture to express how we cherish our children and then use the very same word to describe how much we enjoy M&M's, a movie, or a new pair of shoes. We say that we love our school and love our Lord and with no hesitation. We, in our culture, define *love* by its context within a sentence.

The Bible is far more precise. In Jesus's time (and later

when the New Testament was written), four specific words captured love's distinct biblical meanings. For example, in Greek, *storge* means "family love," how parents and children love one another. The word *eros* (where we get the word *erotic* today) refers to sexual love. The term *philos* means "brotherly love." (This is where we get the name Philadelphia—literally city of brotherly love.) Finally, *agape* describes someone who loves someone who is not deserving. It is a love that doesn't expect anything back. It is a selfless, invincible, never-ending love. It is the way God loves us.

Some people think that to love someone like that (agape) means letting others run over us, take advantage of us, or even somehow abuse us. Agape doesn't mean that. No, agape means being willing to step into someone's messy life, even those who hurt us, and not seek revenge but call them to a better, holier way of life. And when Jesus tells His followers to love their enemies, that's the picture He uses. We are to agape them the way God first loved us. Now how does that happen? How do we learn to love those—to agape those—around us?

AGAPE COMES WHEN WE CONNECT WITH CHRIST

First, we need to see that Jesus gave this command to love (agape) others to His followers, not to unbelievers. Jesus only commands His followers to agape others because it is impossible to love your enemies without the love of Christ within you.

A few Christmases ago, my wife and I began decorating our home. I must say we go all out. For us, it is fun to celebrate the arrival of our Savior with a home that reflects what's in our hearts. The part of holiday decorating that I don't look forward to is hanging lights on the eight-foot Christmas tree. That's because I'm too cheap to buy new tree lights each year, so we use old strings. It never fails; the lights will work for a while, and then suddenly one or more of the strings go dark. Then it's time to start checking each light bulb on the line and, if unsuccessful, removing the glass bulbs and candy canes and replacing that defective string with another. It seems every year I spend hours trying to figure out how to replace or repair the old Christmas tree lights. One Christmas, I put up the tree and hung the lights when an old string already on the tree began to go on and off. I checked the plug; it was securely inserted into the extension cord. Next, I started the tedious work of replacing one bulb at a time to see if I could get the lights to stay on. I must have worked for thirty minutes on that one string and never could get it to work. As I was about to give up, I noticed that our chocolate brown Lab (named Hershey) had gone behind the Christmas tree to sleep. Soon I discovered that our eighty-pound dog had leaned against the extension cord and unplugged it from the wall. And let me tell you that no matter how many lights I replaced on that string, none of them were going to work if they weren't plugged into the power source.

It is the same with our capacity to love one another. On our own, we don't possess the spiritual resources to love others as Christ has called us to love. As we stay connected to Christ (our power source), His love flows through us to those he places in our path. That's how we love those who have hurt us in some way; within our hearts, we can't love like Jesus. Only when Jesus's love overflows in our lives can we fulfill Jesus's command to love. Our job is to abide in Him and stay connected to the One who both commands us to love and provides the means to do so.

AGAPE IS A PROCESS

The second thing we need to understand about loving like Jesus is that it isn't an emotion; it is a matter of surrender. There will be much more on this later in the book. But for now, know it is a process of surrendering each part of our lives.

Yohanna Katanacho[4] is a professor in a Christian school in Jerusalem and pastors a small church there. As a Palestinian living in Israel, he is persecuted by some Palestinians who see him as a traitor. The Israelis also oppress him because he is not Jewish. He writes that the most challenging kind of persecution comes from Israeli soldiers. The soldiers are looking for potential terrorists and have the authority to stop any Palestinian any time and detain them for minutes, hours, or days without due process. As a Christian, he knows that Christ had called him to love all those who persecuted him, but he struggled mightily with loving those who made his life so hard. He said he tried, really tried, to feel love for these soldiers when being stopped, but the feeling never really came. After one stop, he went to his home to pray. He told God that he didn't feel any love for those soldiers, and he had tried, but it just wasn't there. And then he

---

[4] https://www.sermoncentral.com/sermon-illustrations/79730/love-of-the-disciples-by-sermoncentral.

said that as he prayed, he realized something. Agape kind of love isn't an emotion; it is a decision to obey. He decided that even though he didn't feel love for the soldiers, he would show love anyway. So he started carrying copies of a flyer with him, written in Hebrew and English, with a quotation from Isaiah 53 and the words "Real Love" printed across the top. Every time a soldier stopped him, he handed him both his ID card and the flyer. Because the quote came from the Hebrew scriptures, the soldier usually asked him about it before letting him go. So then he would share his faith in Christ. After several months of doing this, Yohanna said he noticed his feelings toward the soldiers had changed. And now I quote him.

> I was surprised, you know? It was a process, but I didn't pay attention to that process. My older feelings were not there anymore. I would pass in the same street, see the same soldiers as before, but now find myself praying, "Lord, let them stop me so that I can share with them the love of Christ."

Surrendering in obedience to Jesus was the key. Once that happened, Jesus began to change Yohanna's heart.

LOOK FOR YOUR FATHER'S FACE

Do you see how this works? First, we must make sure we are connected to our power source. That's Christ. Then we must make the decision (even if we don't feel it) to love those around us. Then slowly, almost imperceptibly, as we trust

Christ's command to love our enemies, something miraculous happens; the Holy Spirit begins to change us. Ultimately, even our feelings will change. Finally, we will start to see all people (even former adversaries) as fellow children of God.

Max Lucado tells a great story about two brothers.[5] One was named Daniel, and he was a big, muscular man. His brother conned him out of a business deal. He vowed that if he ever saw him again, he would break his neck. A few months later, Daniel became a Christ follower. Even so, he couldn't forgive his brother. One day, the inevitable encounter took place on a busy avenue. Daniel described what happened.

> I saw him, but he didn't see me. I felt my fists clench and my face get hot. My initial impulse was to grab him around the throat and choke the life out of him. But as I looked into his face, my anger began to melt. For as I saw him, I saw the image of our father. I saw my father's eyes. I saw my father's look. I saw my father's expression. And as I saw my father in his face, my enemy once again became my brother.

The scoundrel brother soon found himself wrapped in those big arms of his brother in a bear hug. The two stood in the middle of the river of people and wept. Daniel's words bear

---

[5] Max Lucado, *The Applause of Heaven* (Word, 1990), 114–116; submitted by Lee Eclov, Vernon Hills, Illinois.

repeating. "When I saw the image of my father in his face, my enemy became my brother."

And that's the final step in learning to love our enemies. It is when we look them in the face and no longer see enemies. Who we see is an image of our Heavenly Father.

Someone once said, "You can measure the love you have in your heart by the way you love those you like the least." So true. Love, agape love, changes everything. This is deep stuff, and it is not quickly learned. But for those who follow Christ, it is not an option; it is worth the journey.

CHAPTER 4

DECIDING TO LOVE

YOU PROBABLY COULDN'T tell it by looking at me, but I love to work out. To me, a great morning begins with coffee and prayer, and then I'm off to the gym for a forty-five-minute workout before returning home to start my day. This regimen is rarely disturbed, except two times a year. The first is immediately after New Year's Day when people with renewed resolutions to get fit pack the gym. It is so crowded that I sometimes would have to wait in line for a stationary bike. By February, those with such great intentions are no longer working the machines or lifting weights. All those men and women wearing the latest workout styles somehow disappear each year until next January. The only other time the gym is overcapacity is in early spring in what we in Florida call the beginning of "bikini season." This annual event happens in April or May when it is warm enough to return to the beach. That's when beach walkers, surfers, and sunbathers discover that last summer's bikinis or trunks don't fit as they remember. So into the gym they fly, sweating and lifting and stretching, hoping to see the return of their beach body. This flurry of activity from these twenty- and thirtysomethings lasts a couple of weeks, and then the gym returns to us, the old guys and gals and a few other regulars.

Now I know that everyone who joins a gym fully intends to improve their health. But the truth is intentions and commitments are not the same things. When Jesus commands us to love others as He first loved us, it takes more than good intentions for that to happen. Listen to this command from our Lord (John 15:9–17):

> As the Father has loved me, so I have loved you; abide in my love. If you keep my commandments, you will abide in my love, just as I have kept my Father's commandments and abide in his love. I have said these things to you so that my joy may be in you, and that your joy may be complete. This is my commandment, that you love one another as I have loved you. No one has greater love than this, to lay down one's life for one's friends. You are my friends if you do what I command you. I do not call you

servants any longer, because the servant does not know what the master is doing; but I have called you friends, because I have made known to you everything—that I have heard from my Father. You did not choose me but I chose you. And I appointed you to go and bear fruit, fruit that will last, so that the Father will give you whatever you ask Him in my name. I am giving you these commands so that you may love one another.

The best definition of love (agape) that I know comes from 1 Corinthians 13. First, read this paraphrased version of verses 4–7. This is how the Bible defines *love:*

Love is patient; love is kind; love is not envious or boastful or arrogant or rude. Love does not insist on its own way; love is not irritable or resentful; love does not rejoice in wrongdoing, but love rejoices in the truth. Love bears all things, believes all things, hopes all things, endures all things.

Since scripture teaches that God is the author and very embodiment of love, I invite you to reread it, but this time, I want to exchange the word *love* with the name *Jesus.*

Jesus is patient; Jesus is kind; Jesus is not envious or boastful or arrogant or rude. Jesus does not insist on His own way; Jesus is not irritable or resentful; Jesus does not rejoice in wrongdoing, but Jesus rejoices in the truth. Jesus bears all things, believes all things, hopes all things, endures all things.

Now let us see how loving we are. Read this text for the third time, but this time, insert your name in the blanks, where Jesus's name had previously been.

_____ is patient; _____ is kind; _____ is not envious or boastful or arrogant or rude. _____ does not insist on his/her own way; _____ is not irritable or resentful; _____ does not rejoice in wrongdoing, but _____ rejoices in the truth. _____ bears all things, believes all things, hopes all things, endures all things.

For me, this shows me how much more I need to grow in love.

I believe that there are four levels of love. The first is to love someone who loves you back like a family member, a husband/wife relationship, or maybe just a very close friend. This is the most accessible kind of love; anyone can love someone who loves you back. Almost everyone achieves this level at some point in their lives.

The second level is loving a friend or colleague. This person could be a neighbor, a friend at church, or someone you work with regularly. You aren't "like a family member close," but God has given you a deep caring about their well-being. Most people have this level two kind of love with at least a couple of people.

The third level gets a bit more challenging. That is to love someone you don't know. It means tithing or maybe giving up that ridiculously priced cup of coffee to support missionaries who will serve people we will never meet. Our hearts break when we see a TV advertisement of a ministry asking for money where children are shown starving and flies are swarming around them. Yet most people just change the channel. It is easier to do that than love someone halfway around the world. Level three love is what leads us to support evangelism and the ministry of caring around the world. Someone once said that evangelism is one beggar telling another beggar where the food is, and if we genuinely love the world, we will want them to know the Bread of Life!

Level four love is the toughest. Not many people get there. That is loving an enemy or someone who has hurt you. It is not retaliating when someone wrongs you. It is taking the high road, even when people are stabbing you in the back. That's the way Jesus loves.

EV Hill was the minister of a church in LA during the racial riots in the 1960s. He took a strong stand against rioters and looters who were destroying other people's property. For that, he got all kinds of threats against his church and even some death threats. One evening the phone rang, and EV's wife noticed that after her husband hung up the phone, he was very solemn and quiet. She asked him what had happened, and at first, he was reluctant to tell her. But finally, she pried it out of him. The caller said that he was going to blow up his car with EV in it. They embraced one another, they cried, and they prayed.

Finally, they went to bed, and the next morning, EV got up and went into the kitchen. He could not find his wife and noticed the car was gone. He was very alarmed and was about to start calling friends and neighbors when his wife walked in the back door. She said, "I decided to drive the car around the block to make sure it was safe for you this morning." From that moment, EV Hill never asked or even wondered about his wife's love for him. He saw it with his own eyes.

Now my guess is that every one of us would do what his wife did for our spouse, children, or family member. That's level one love. Most of us would do this for a close friend or colleague. That's level two. How about a stranger? Would we do that for someone we didn't know? Not many of us are at level three. Would we do such a loving thing for an enemy? Jesus loved at that fourth level, and He wants us to learn to love at that level too.

CHAPTER 5

LEARNING TO LOVE LIKE JESUS

I F WE WANT to love like Jesus, we must become more like Jesus. That isn't something we can do by sheer will, by sacrifice, or by self-flagellation. Loving like Jesus requires the Holy Spirit to do something in us that we cannot do for ourselves. Paul writes in 1 Thessalonians 5:16–24,

> Rejoice always, pray without ceasing, give thanks in all circumstances; for this is the will of God in Christ Jesus for you. Do not quench the Spirit. Do not despise the words of prophets, but test everything; hold fast to what is good;

abstain from every form of evil. May the God of peace himself sanctify you entirely; and may your spirit and soul and body be kept sound and blameless at the coming of our Lord Jesus Christ. The one who calls you is faithful, and he will do this.

Scripture is clear; it is the work of the Holy Spirit that makes us more like Jesus. It is a lifetime of the Spirit teaching, encouraging, and empowering us we follow our Lord. On this lifelong journey of faith, we slowly become more like our journey's leader. Do we have a part to play in our sanctification? Absolutely! Just as scripture teaches us to pray, even though God already knows everything before we utter a word, we too are invited to be part of the sanctification process. Paul tells us in 1 Thessalonians 5:16–22 that followers should rejoice, pray, be thankful, and resist evil. Those things don't sanctify us in and of themselves but are tools that the Holy Spirit uses to grow us. Let me illustrate. Years ago, Will Willimon was the chaplain at Duke University. He tells of a time he spotted a young coed at Duke walking with a handsome, young man through the Duke Gardens.[6] Willimon knew her from class, and she was bright and very pretty, so when he saw her next, he boldly asked if she was in love.

"Why do you ask that?" she asked.

---

[6] *Preaching Journal* (Jackson, TN Preaching Resources, Inc.), May–June 1999, pages 47–48.

"Well, I saw you in the gardens arm-in-arm
with a young man. It's such a romantic place. I
just wondered if you were in love."
She answered, "No, I was not there because I
am in love. I was there because I want to be in
love."

In other words, she was intentionally putting herself in a
place where love could happen. That's how we assist the Holy
Spirit in our sanctification. When we are thankful, joyous, go
on mission trips, pray regularly, and worship consistently, we
put ourselves in places where the Spirit can grow us. We don't
do the sanctifying, but we do play a part. Our job is to put
ourselves in places where we are available and teachable.

A few years ago, I talked to a parishioner who rarely came
to church and never attended men's meetings or Sunday school.
He spent Sunday mornings playing golf. One evening we ran
into each other at a party. We were doing the typical party
small talk when he told me he was sorry he wasn't in church
more. Apparently, he felt the need to explain his situation. He
shared that he worked hard all week, Saturdays were family
days, and Sundays were his only free day to play golf. As if to
justify himself more, he went on to tell me that he could pray
just as well on a golf course as he could in church.

I agreed with him. I told him that people could worship
God on a golf course, which seemed to surprise him. Then I
went on.

Yes, you can also pray just as well in a bar, or sunning at the beach, or on a bass boat as you can in church, but when was the last time you saw that happen? Sure it is possible to worship anywhere, but my experience is that just because it is possible doesn't mean it ever happens.

He was in church the following Sunday. The point is we, as believers, have a role to play in our own sanctification. And that is to place ourselves in an environment where the Spirit has room in our lives to teach, prune, encourage, and grow us. We need space in our busy lives where we can turn off our phones and Wi-Fi and attune ourselves to God's voice and open our lives to the powerful words of restoration as the Lord speaks into our hearts. If we want to love like Jesus, we must make room in our lives for the Spirit to work.

A PATHWAY TO GROWTH

When we become Christ followers, the Spirit begins the sanctification process. How does that work? What are the steps in the process? Are there mile markers along the way to show our progress? How do we know if we are maturing in our faith and becoming more like Jesus? Jesus has provided such a pathway. We call them the Beatitudes. The Beatitudes are some of the most familiar words in the New Testament—and some of the most misunderstood.

Dr. William Arthur[7] tells of a man named Jake Wurm, who walked down a California beach about four decades ago. Life had not been easy for Jake; his business failed, he had no job, and he was walking down the beach just kicking up the sand while waiting for a job interview later that day. As Jake walked, he noticed a bottle half-buried in the sand. He looked down at the bottle and noticed something was in it. So he kicked the bottle, and sure enough, it contained a note. He picked up the bottle, uncorked it, and read the letter.

> To avoid confusion, I leave my entire estate to the lucky person who finds this bottle and to my attorney, Barry Cohen, share and share alike.
> Daisy Alexander
> June 20, 1937

The name of Daisy Alexander didn't mean anything to Jake, and he figured it was just a joke, so he didn't think much about it. Later he told a friend about the note, and his friend told Jake that he had just read something in the newspaper about someone named Daisy Alexander. So Jake decided to investigate. What Jake found was that Daisy Alexander was the heiress to the Singer Sewing Machine fortune. She had a net worth of about $14 million. It turned out that she was an eccentric old lady who lived in England. People saw her often

---

[7] Story told by Dr. Arthur in sermon "Uncorking a Fortune," in Shandon Presbyterian Church, Columbia, SC, 1986, and retold by Frank Harrington in sermon "When Sugar Comes off the Pill" at Peachtree Presbyterian Church, Atlanta, GA, June 1995.

drop bottles in the water. She died in 1939 at the age of eighty-one with no will.

Oceanographers believe that after Daisy Alexander dropped that bottle in the river, it must have washed down the Thames River, into the English Channel, and through the North Sea and Bering Strait into the North Atlantic. Then currents took it around the tip of South America and finally up to California. The experts estimate that it took ten to fifteen years for the bottle to make the trip and then lay there on the beach—a fortune waiting to be claimed.

When the Jake Wurm story first got out, I wonder how other beachcombers in the area felt. How many people must have seen the old, half-buried bottle and thought it was nothing more than garbage that had washed up onshore. Think of the people who stepped over the bottle and missed the fortune, unaware of the treasure within.

The Beatitudes are like that lost treasure. For some, Jesus's words are overlooked because, on the surface, they appear incomprehensible; others find them confusing or even contradictory. For some readers, these words are so familiar that they have lost their importance to us. Still, others are new to following Jesus and have never studied this life-giving message. Today, many believers are like those California beachcombers and have stepped over these words of Christ, not understanding that there is a treasure to be claimed. These words of Jesus form a rich picture of the pathway to a mature Christian life and the power to love like Jesus.

Before we dig into the Beatitudes, there are a couple of

things we need to understand. First, each Beatitude begins with the word "blessed." We use the word *blessed* in all kinds of ways today. We bless people when they sneeze. We say a blessing before we eat. My grandmother's favorite phrase, when hearing something went wrong with someone, was "Bless their hearts." So blessings mean all kinds of things today.

In Greek, the word *blessed* (the Greek word is *makarios)* is translated as "happy." The Greek's used the term to depict someone who enjoyed wealth and privilege.[8] Matthew used the word in a new way. When Matthew said, "Blessed is the …" he isn't describing people with material wealth. Matthew is saying that those who live like Jesus have a different kind of wealth. According to Matthew, those who are "blessed" are fabulously rich spiritually because they live life with Jesus as our Shepherd. Blessed people are women and men who live as faithful followers of Jesus Christ. For our purposes, I would translate "blessed" as "one who walks closely with Jesus."

The second thing I want us to understand is that the Beatitudes help paint a picture of a believer with a mature faith. For many, we never had a mature believer mentor us or walk with us in our faith journey. We just learned how to follow Jesus through trial and error.

When Virginia (my wife of more than four decades) and I

---

[8] In Greek usage, makarios came to refer to the elite, the upper crust, the wealthy people. It referred to people who had such wealth that they could live without worry of food, shelter, or clothing. To be blessed, you had no worries about the basic needs of life and were very rich and powerful. http://www.crossmarks.com/brian/allsaintb.htm.

were first married, we were both believers, and we both wanted to have a Christian marriage. But honestly, we were young, and at least for me, I didn't know what a Christian marriage looked like. In my family growing up, my dad was a road warrior (traveled five days a week on business), so I never really saw him lead our family spiritually. I didn't have a model to follow, and I remember praying that the Lord would show me a biblical view of marriage. Jesus didn't send me a book or a video series; God sent me a godly boss.

This guy loved his wife and kids differently from what I had ever seen before. This dad told me how he made time to have a date night with his wife each week. He told me how he spent individual time (he called it dating his daughters) with his three daughters every week. He asked his son to pick out a sport they could do together, and for many years, he and his son would play that sport. I saw his church involvement, how he spent his money, and even how he spoke to his family members. Most of all, I saw his faithfulness and love and his passion for Jesus. Through this older man, I got a picture of a healthy Christian marriage. Jesus used him to show me the way. What a gift! For those of us who didn't have a spiritual mentor, Jesus has provided one for us. That's what the Beatitudes do for our spiritual lives. They are a guide to how we start our journey with the Lord. As the years go by, they provide benchmarks along the way. They point us to holy attributes that Jesus wants to place in our lives.

For many years, I believed that the Beatitudes could best be understood as a spiritual ladder. The first wrung of the ladder was our conversion (and an infantile faith) and culminated with sturdy spiritual roots that can withstand even persecution. Just as one climbs a ladder by starting at the bottom and stepping from one rung to the next, a believer will begin at the first Beatitude and make their way up the Beatitude ladder one step at a time. Over time, my view of the Beatitudes changed. I learned from my own life; I didn't climb this spiritual ladder just once. But the Lord would have me climb it over and over again, each time laying bare deeper parts of my personality and character traits. It seemed each time I climbed the ladder, the deeper He probed my heart and soul.

C. S. Lewis, my favorite writer, captures this sanctification process in a scene from one of his books, *The Voyage of the Dawn Treader*[9] (from his book series The Chronicles of Narnia). In this book, we find a very unlikeable young boy named Eustace. In this memorable scene, Eustace steals a gold armband and puts it on, only to discover that his greed turns him into a dragon. The more he transforms into a dragon, the more the armband becomes excruciatingly tight on his dragon foot. One night, amid his pain and frustration, Eustace encounters a huge lion named Aslan (who represents Christ in the series). Aslan tells the boy to follow him to a high mountain well.

Eustace longs to bathe his aching dragon foot in the cool water, but Aslan tells him he must undress first. It seems silly to Eustace because dragons don't wear clothes, but then he remembers that dragons, like snakes, cast their skins. So

[9] C. S. Lewis, *The Voyage of the Dawn Treader*, book 3 in the series Chronicles of Narnia (Collier Books, NYC, 1952), 73–90.

Eustace scratches his skin, and the scales begin falling off. Soon, his whole skin peels away. But when he puts his foot in the water, he sees that it is just as rough and scaly as before. He continues scratching at the second dragon skin and a third skin, only to realize there is yet another underneath. Finally, the lion says, "You will have to let me do it for you." Eustace is afraid of the lion's claws but desperate to get in the water, so he consents. The first tear is painfully deep as the lion begins to peel away the dragon skin. Surely death will follow, Eustace believes. Finally, Aslan completely removed the dragon skin, returning Eustace to his human form. With the gnarled mess of dragon skin now cut away, the majestic lion holds Eustace and throws him into the water. Initially, the water stings, but soon Eustice says it is perfectly delicious. And then he realizes that he can swim without pain, for he's a boy again.

That picture of Aslan tearing away the dragon skin is an excellent picture of what it looks like to be sanctified. It is a pruning, a tearing away, a surrender, and finally submitting to Christ's spiritual restoration. Often that process is painful, sometimes joyous, but it is always good to feel the hand of God reshaping us.

If you are ready to let Jesus remake you, let us look at how He might use these Beatitudes to renew our hearts and lives. There are eight Beatitudes, and they are found in Matthew 5:1–12.

When Jesus saw the crowds,—he went up the mountain; and after he sat down, his disciples came to him. Then he began to speak, and taught them, saying:

Blessed are the poor in spirit, for theirs is the kingdom of heaven.

Blessed are those who mourn, for they will be comforted.

Blessed are the meek, for they will inherit the earth.

Blessed are those who hunger and thirst for righteousness, for they will be filled.

Blessed are the merciful, for they will receive mercy.

Blessed are the pure in heart, for they will see God.

Blessed are the peacemakers, for they shall be called children of God.

Blessed are those who have been persecuted for the sake of righteousness, for theirs is the kingdom of heaven. Rejoice and be glad, for your reward is great in heaven, for in the same way they persecuted the prophets who were before you.

"BLESSED ARE THE POOR IN SPIRIT ..."

THE FIRST BEATITUDE comes to us in Matthew 5:3. "Blessed are the poor in spirit for theirs is the kingdom of God." When people hear this phrase "Blessed are the poor in spirit," many think that Jesus is saying that somehow God blesses us, or we are on the right track with God when we are economically poor.[10] Some will even go so far as to say that this text shows a divine preference for those who suffer financially. This Beatitude has been so misunderstood through the ages that in AD 300, the Roman emperor Julian heard these words of Jesus and sarcastically ordered that Christians should have their property confiscated so they could enter the kingdom of God. The emperor's act said far more about him than it did about Jesus's words. In short, this teaching has nothing to do with the amount of money someone might or might not have.

Some have thought that being poor in spirit refers to people whose lives have not turned out well. Jesus's message is one of consolation to those whose careers or marriages ended up on the rocks. Some believed that Jesus was saying to those who have been victims of the hardships of this world that God still loved them, and even though this life might have ended up in the ditch, the next life (in heaven) will be much better.

Still others believed that this text refers to those who are depressed, wounded, and joyless. They assert that Jesus's

---

[10] It is interesting to note that when John the Baptist was looking for confirmation of Jesus's divinity, Jesus responded by paraphrasing Isaiah 61:1–2. Jesus says in Luke 7:22 (NRSV),

> And he answered them, "Go and tell John what you have seen and heard: the blind receive their sight, the lame walk, the lepers are cleansed, the deaf hear, the dead are raised, the poor have good news brought to them."

Are the poor Jesus refers to those who struggle with resource depravation, or is Jesus referring to the spiritually poor (those who know they need a Savior)? It is apparent to me that Isaiah 61 refers to those in material poverty while Jesus's statement is about spiritual and economic poverty.

message was that there may not be joy now, but there will be an abundance in the life to come. But again, this text is more than a promise of future happiness.

I am convinced that being poor in spirit refers to all people, not just those who suffer from financial trials, depression, experience personal failure, or live a joyless life. This text is much more universal than limiting it to a few specific groups. This text, I believe, is referring to the spiritual condition of the human heart.

THREE MAJOR CHARACTERISTICS OF A HEART THAT IS POOR IN SPIRIT

Only when we come to grips with our own sinfulness will we begin to see a need for a Savior. Most people, even many Christians, believe that our sinfulness is a matter of bad decisions, poor parenting by those who raised us, or societal pressures and temptations. Indeed, circumstances play a part in our godless decisions, but scripture is clear that sin is more than a series of bad choices. It is a condition of the heart. Romans 5:22–23 says, "For there is no distinction, since all have sinned and fall short of the glory of God." And no matter how hard we try, how hard we work, or how many promises we make to ourselves, sin is ever-present in our lives. The apostle Paul (Romans 7:18–20) said this about sin in his own life:

> For I know that nothing good dwells within me,
> that is, in my flesh. I can will what is right, but
> I cannot do it. For I do not do the good I want,

but the evil I do not want is what I do. Now if I
do what I do not want, it is no longer I that do
it, but sin that dwells within me.

Paul struggled with sin just as you and I do. His sinful nature
was so real to him that Paul wrote in Romans 7:24, "Wretched
man that I am! Who will rescue me from this body of death?"

Some think that to rid ourselves of sinfulness, we must try
harder to be moral and kinder or have purer thoughts. Others
believe that more education or better parenting skills can
remove our sinful nature. Ephesians 2:8–10 says that defeating
sin isn't something we can do. Only Jesus can defeat sin.

For by grace you have been saved through faith,
and this is not your own doing; it is the gift of
God—not the result of works, so that no one
may boast. For we are what he has made us,
created in Christ Jesus for good works, which
God prepared beforehand to be our way of life.

Sin is a spiritual heart disease that we all struggle with and
can only be defeated by the cross of Jesus Christ and the renewal
of our hearts by the Holy Spirit. It is when we, as believers, grasp
that concept and live as people purchased by the love and blood
of Jesus that we become poor in spirit. To be clear, being poor
in spirit is the recognition of our need for a Savior.

When Virginia and I were first married, we were living
in Tampa, Florida. Virginia was still in college, and I was a
trainee on Young Life staff. At that time, we were trying to

live on about $540 per month, most of which I was responsible for raising. That was a real exercise of faith for us. We lived off peanut butter and jelly sandwiches for days at a time. Bologna was a treat! We made Christmas presents for our family because we had no money to buy gifts. We were always glad when my dad came to town on a business trip because he would take us out to a nice restaurant for dinner. One afternoon, I played basketball with some of the Young Life leaders and found a $5 bill in the parking lot. One of the guys saw me pick up the bill and said, "Hey, Robert, why don't you buy us some Cokes?" I knew I couldn't because that money was needed to help buy food or gas for the car.

One day Virginia purchased a ham that she was going to cook for dinner that evening. The ham was big enough to give us leftovers for the rest of the week. I got home that evening and found our little duplex full of smoke. When Virginia heard me come through the door, she ran toward me with tears coming down her face. The only words she could get out were "I burned the ham. I burned the ham." It wasn't just burned a little. It looked like a giant hockey puck—hard, round, and black. I have never liked ham much after that.

What would we do now? We had no money to buy more food; it looked like it would be another peanut butter and jelly sandwich week. Not too many days had passed when we got our bank statement, and when we reconciled it (which took about twenty-eight seconds because it was essentially all zeros), we discovered the bank had made a mistake in our favor of $50. Boy, we needed the money, but we knew we had to be honest so we went to the bank the next day and told the teller of their mistake. She looked up the deposit and said, "It is a cash deposit in your account. It's yours. Just enjoy it." We were rich!

For the next year, money would show up in our account. It was never a lot, sometimes $15, sometimes $25, sometimes more. But what was amazing to us was every time there was a big bill, tuition was due, or the car needed work, more cash would show up. Each time we would report it, and they would act like it was a mystery.

Finally, after one of the more significant gifts showed up, I asked one of the bankers, "It's the same person putting cash in our account each time, isn't it?" He just smiled and said, "Enjoy it!" And we did. We never found out who it was, but we had our suspicions.[11]

These anonymous cash gifts were simple, unearned gifts from someone who loved us, and all we had to do was accept them. No one had to convince us of our needs. To this day (forty-four years later), we still talk about the hockey puck ham and the mysterious gifts.

Someone poor in spirit is like that. People poor in spirit know they need outside help. Poor in spirit people know they are spiritually broken and stand in need of Christ's love and grace in their lives. Poor in spirit people accept Jesus's gift of life not because we are good or deserving but because Jesus is good.

Second, poor in spirit people are filled with humility. We

---

[11] We always suspected it was the parents of one YL student that we had a special relationship with. That was confirmed for us in 2020 (some four decades later).

have all met people who wear their faith like a badge, like it is something that they want to show off. But someone poor in spirit wants their life to point not to themselves but to Christ.

A while back, it was reported that a man was standing in line at an airport check-in counter. He was well dressed, and by the look on his face, it was apparent he was anxious. Ahead of him were others who had also arrived late for the flight, and everyone's anxiety level went up when they saw the door to the jetway close.

When he realized he was about to miss that flight, he pushed his way to the front of the line and said, "Excuse me, miss, but I need to get on this flight." "Yes, sir, so do the rest of the people who are in line in front of you. Now kindly take your place back in line, and we'll help you when it's your turn."

The man didn't move an inch and said to her, "You see, if I don't get this flight, I'm going to miss my meeting, and if you make me miss my appointment, I am going to be very angry with you." So the agent very calmly said, "Sir, we will help you when it is your turn." Now that only made him angrier, and he told her, "Do you know who you are dealing with? I am the vice president of this airline. Do you know who I am?"

Very calmly, the agent picked up the microphone and announced, "Ladies and gentlemen, may I have your attention please? This gentleman at the desk does not seem to know who he is. If anyone can identify him, we would gladly appreciate your assistance." Everyone who was standing in line exploded with applause.

No one likes arrogance in anyone, but it is especially true

when it is spiritual. I was at a gathering of Christians in my community, and a local minister was the keynote speaker. He spent the first five minutes of his message telling the audience how he had gone out of his way to be with us that morning, then went on to tell us what a great basketball player he had been in college, then started listing the achievements of his church (which were many). To be honest, I never heard another word he said that day. He was more interested in us knowing what a great man of God he was than for us to know about the Lord he followed.

Not too long ago, I talked to a waitress who told me how much she hated to work on Sundays. I asked her if it was because she attended church somewhere. She said, "No! I don't go to church, and part of the reason is my experience with church people. Church people fill my restaurant on Sunday afternoons, and they are the most demanding people I serve all week. Then they don't tip well. Some will leave tracks on the table or write on the bill, 'Praying for you.' If those church people loved me, they would be the kindest customers I would have all week and would leave a good tip so I can take care of my children. Instead, no one wants to work Sundays because of the church crowd."

Isn't that sad? Here this waitress only knows of Jesus by how the church crowd treats her on Sunday afternoons. If Christ is like His followers, she wanted nothing to do with Him. What the church crowd did in her restaurant is a perfect picture of spiritual arrogance and a great example of its consequences.

Third, being poor in spirit means being so grateful for what

Jesus has done for us that we are eager to obey His calling on our lives—even if we don't quite understand why. I remember one day at church was particularly busy. I had been in meetings all day long and was on the way back to the church when I stopped by Starbucks to get a cup of ridiculously priced coffee. (OK, I confess, I'm a coffee snob.)

It was a rare cold, rainy day in northeast Florida, and the Starbucks was packed. I am not exaggerating when I say they literally ran out of brewed coffee that afternoon and had to make more. I'm sure it was just a few minutes, but it felt like I waited thirty minutes for my turn with the barista. I finally got my coffee and drove back to church.

The coffee was so hot I could barely take a sip of it. So I let it cool off as I drove. I turned the corner to the old downtown church where I served, and I happened to notice a woman wrapped in blankets huddled in the doorway of our education building (the Williams Building). And as I saw this woman, I thought, *I bet she could use a cup of hot coffee on this cold day.* Then this thought jumped in my head: *Lord, You are not going to tell me to give her my Starbucks coffee, are You?* Then I thought, *No, of course not. She will probably be gone by the time I park and get around the corner.* So I parked, grabbed my briefcase and coffee, and headed to the church entrance.

When I rounded the corner, she was still there. I prayed this very selfish prayer: "Lord, I have to confess that it has been a long day, and I really want this cup of coffee, but if You want me to give it to her, I will. Not because I want to but because You want me to. Lord, make Your will crystal clear."

As I got close to her, I asked her if she was OK, and she said she was OK. The very next thing out of her mouth was "That Starbucks sure looks good on a cold day like today!"

I couldn't believe it! God has a great sense of humor. I told her (giving her another chance to change her mind), "Well, I have already had a couple of sips (honestly hoping she wouldn't want it after I had tasted it). "Oh, that's OK. That won't bother me," she said. It couldn't be any more apparent that the Lord wanted me to give her my Starbucks coffee! I did. Then I went to the church offices and told my assistant what had just happened. We both had a good laugh at what the Lord had done. We didn't laugh because I gave away that silly cup of coffee; we laughed at how our Lord put all these circumstances together so He could supply a great cup of coffee to a homeless lady sitting in front of the church. We laughed because Jesus wanted me to hand-deliver it to her. What a joy it is to be used by the Lord!

Being poor in spirit is knowing you need a Savior; it is living life with humility (pointing others to Him), and last, it is obedience in the big and small things of life. And the reward for all that: Jesus (Matthew 5:3) said "for theirs is the kingdom of heaven." This means we will experience kingdom living like never before. When we embrace our spiritual poverty, we will see Jesus move in our lives and speak to our hearts like never before. The first step in developing a mature walk of faith is recognizing that we have a need for a Savior, and His name is Jesus.

Blessed are the poor in spirit, for theirs
is the kingdom of heaven.

※

BEATITUDE 2

"BLESSED ARE THOSE
WHO MOURN ..."

DO YOU KNOW the name Georgine Johnson?[12] When I first heard of her, she was a woman in her midforties who lived in Cleveland, Ohio. What made Georgine newsworthy was that she participated in a run held in Cleveland. In Cleveland's race, you had a choice; you could do the ten-kilometer (6.2 miles) or the twenty-six-mile marathon. Well, Georgine was just a jogger, not a serious runner, and she decided that the 6.2-mile race was for her. She trained and worked out, and when race day arrived, she was ready. The race was set up so that runners in the 6.2-mile race and twenty-six-mile race started from the

---

[12] https://apnews.com/93316d331cb21a97b534b9426a957222.

same place but fifteen minutes apart. After a few miles, the runners doing the six-mile run would see markers and veer off while the marathoners would keep going.

When the starting gun sounded, Georgine and thousands of other runners took to the street. She felt good as the race progressed, but after a while, she looked around and noticed that the number of runners had significantly decreased. She wondered what was going on. Could she have fallen way behind the other runners? Could it be that she was leading the pack? That's when it hit her! To her horror, she realized that somehow she had missed her turnoff. She was no longer running the six-mile race; she was now running with the marathon runners. Panic set in as she realized she had never run more than six miles at one time in her entire life, much less run a marathon. She had trained and prepared for one race but found herself in the middle of something far more demanding. She was too far down the course to turn back but not sure how long she could keep going.

Have you ever felt like that? Have you found yourself traveling down a road you never expected and wondering, *How in the world did I get where I am today?* Now some side roads in life are beautiful, and we wouldn't have wanted to travel on any other path. But other side roads are painful and difficult. Some difficult side roads are like relationships that we thought would never end, but suddenly there is an illness, tragedy, or divorce. For some, we plan a career only to have our company close, and suddenly we are looking for a new job or even a new career. As youngsters, we are taught to play fair, do the right thing, and things will just work out for the best. But then a drunk driver takes the life of a loved one, and nothing will ever be the same. For some, we plan for retirement, just waiting for the day when there would be time and money to travel and to be with family, and then illness strikes.

That is what happened to a couple in a church I once served. It was a small community with a beautiful bed-and-breakfast not too far from the church. A lovely couple, who were church members, ran it. This couple was so busy on weekends with the guests at their bed-and-breakfast they rarely attended Sunday services. I visited them one day, and they told me how they had both been schoolteachers. They took early retirement to move to our community to set up that bed-and-breakfast. But now, after many years of running the inn, they were going to sell it and live the dream. Being teachers, they never had enough money to travel, so now they would see the country. They wanted to go to every national park in America. They had worked so hard their entire lives and now were going to do the things they could never do before. I went to the retirement party and celebrated their marvelous achievement.

One week later, the husband had a devastating stroke that permanently paralyzed him and left him in a vegetative state. At first, we were hopeful he would improve. But as the days turned into weeks, we realized he would never recover. He couldn't even talk. He would live in a nursing home for the rest of his life. I remember visiting him and his wife at the facility. Unable to speak, he would lie there and cry. There would be no travel or visiting family and friends; no dream would come true. They never made it back to church. I met with his wife, who told me through her tears that life was not supposed to be like this. This wasn't fair, and she didn't know how she could go on. But she wouldn't abandon him. She was faithful to the end. They were running a race they never wanted or expected.

All of us will one day have to deal with pain and suffer significant losses in life. Jesus knew that and spoke to that human condition in the second Beatitude. He says, "Blessed are those who mourn, for they will be comforted" (Matthew 5:4).

Now to understand this phrase, we will need to define some words. First, we have said previously that the word *blessed* in Greek means to be happy or even wealthy. In Hebrew, it has a completely different meaning. In Hebrew, the term *blessed* comes from the word *barak,* which is best translated as "to kneel." So in Hebrew, the image of one who is blessed is someone down on their knees, head bowed, humbly praying. Being blessed isn't about being fortunate. It is about kneeling before a faithful and loving God, knowing that God is always faithful in good times and trials. When the writer Zig Ziglar[13] tragically lost his daughter, he wrote these words:

> The longest 24 hours of my life were those after my daughter's death. When making the funeral arrangements with her husband and his parents, I had to listen to a salesman who was an incessant talker and who told us 30 times

---

[13] See http://www.bpnews.net/2183/zig-ziglar-pens-8216confessions8217-on-grief-after-daughter8217s-d for more information.

he wasn't a salesman. Twice while we were making decisions about her casket and burial, I had to leave the room; I simply couldn't handle him. The night before, I had hallucinated. Half asleep, half awake, I kept thinking my daughter was wondering when her daddy was going to come get her. The next morning I took a walk and was praying and crying the whole way.

That was when the Holy Spirit showed up in a way that only God could. In his heart of hearts, Ziglar knew that his daughter was in the presence of God. He knew she was safe and with her Savior. The peace that Jesus promised to give (John 14:27) came to Ziglar at that moment. He knew that Jesus was all he needed, and Ziglar's job was to "keep walking. Keep talking. Keep praying. Keep crying."

Ziglar's experience with grief is one we all will experience one day. As Ziglar prayed, we see a beautiful picture of what the Hebrew understanding of being blessed is. It is kneeling before God, praying, and sharing our pain and struggles, and God responding by coming close in the midst of our suffering with words of life and words of hope.

When Jesus said, "Blessed are those who mourn," He was saying that those who kneel before God, those who turn to God in prayer in times of trouble, will be comforted. What does it mean to be comforted by God? The word *comfort* comes from two Latin words: *cum,* which means "with," and *fortis,* which means "strength." (This is where we get the words *fort* and *fortress* today.) So the term *comfort* means "with strength." Here Christ gives us an encouraging promise that those who kneel before God in times of trouble and grief will receive new strength.

I began this section by telling you about Georgine Johnson, a woman who accidentally found herself running a marathon. She completed that race. She found the strength to complete a race she had never trained to run. Somehow she had the strength to take one more step. For all who find themselves enduring a race they never prepared for, for all who have gone too far and can't turn back, and for all who aren't sure you have enough strength to take the next step, remember Christ's promise: to give you His strength, when yours is depleted. In His strength, you can always take the next step.

Blessed are those who mourn, for they will be comforted.

"BLESSED ARE THE MEEK ..."

STEVE BROWN TELLS a story of a damsel in distress in an old Western movie. She was all alone in a horse-drawn wagon. Suddenly something spooked the horses, and like all teams of horses in old Westerns, the horses began running down that trail like their tails were on fire. The situation looked hopeless for our damsel. Then, from out of the hills, rode the hero on his white steed.

In just seconds, he caught up to the wagon and lept from his horse onto the backs of the team of horses pulling the wagon. Of course, he stopped the horses just in the nick of time, avoiding mayhem and disaster. The heroine was so grateful; she looked at her hero with stars in her eyes, and they embraced. With a sense of relief, she said to the cowboy, "I trusted God with my life until the reins broke."

Now when I first heard this story, my questions were, "If she trusted God until the reins broke, was she ever really trusting in God at all? Or had she actually put her trust in the reins and her ability to control the situation?" Sometimes the reins have to break in life, and we lose control before realizing where we are placing our trust.

That's the message of the third Beatitude, "Blessed are the meek." What Christ was saying to his disciples (and to us today) is that real life, real direction, and real purpose only come when we stop clutching the reins of our lives and hand them over to Jesus Christ.

So often, we think that when Christ said, "Blessed are the meek," He was telling His followers to be spineless wimps and that we are to let people run over us and we are to have no opinion, no feelings, and no backbone. But being meek and being milquetoast have nothing to do with each other.

The Greek word for *meek* is *praus,* and it was a word used to describe the training of wild animals, like military horses. It is the training process by which the horse is caught and then taught to obey the trainer's commands. The horse doesn't hold the reins. The trainer does. And when the trainer pulls the reins to the left, the horse learns to go left. When the trainer pulls the reins to the right, the horse learns to go right. When the trainer pulls the reins back, the horse learns to stop. A good trainer never destroys the horse's personality, makes the horse physically weak, or even breaks the horse's spirit. No, the trainer's goal is to bring the power and strength of the horse under control.

I read recently how Arabian horses were trained. Hour after hour, day after day, the stallions were taught to obey their master and to trust him without hesitation. Each trainer would have a whistle, and at the sound of the whistle, the stallions were trained to stop whatever they were doing and come immediately to their trainer.

After weeks of training, the horses were placed in a corral halfway up a hillside. At the bottom of the hill was a beautiful pond with crystal-blue waters. The stallions stayed in the corral for several hours in the hot desert sun with no water until their thirst made them almost frantic.

Then the trainer would go to the top of the hill, and the horses were released from the corral. Of course, the horses immediately headed for the pond. Just before they reached the water, the trainer would blow his whistle. The praus (meek) horses would quickly turn away from the pond and go to the trainer. They were considered well-trained. Those horses who went on to the pond to take a drink were deemed not ready and were returned for more training.

That is a beautiful picture of what it means to be meek. Being meek doesn't mean being weak; it means strength under control. It is when we hand the reins of life over to Christ and come under His command that two significant things happen.

First, sanctification begins. When we turn the reins of our lives over to Christ, He becomes our Savior and our spiritual trainer. In short, Jesus will change us. When you follow Christ, you will not be the same person a year from now that you are today. In five years, you will be a different person from who you are a year from now.

In my former church, there was a freshman in college. He was in a horrific car accident, and fortunately, everyone would eventually recover. But his right foot was shattered in the accident. The doctors told him and his family that it would take at least three surgeries for his foot to heal, maybe more. It was going to be a long and painful recovery with months of rehabilitation.

Now that college student could have said, "Hey, I don't want to go through all that. My foot is OK just the way it is. Who wants to go through all those operations? Who wants to go through all that pain? No surgeries. I like my foot the way it is." Now he didn't say any of those things. He was ready to do whatever it took to get back to college with his friends. He knew there would be some tough days ahead, but he was willing to pay that price to get well. Spiritual growth and maturity are like that. It is never easy to grow, and sometimes it is downright painful. Change, spiritual or otherwise, always is.

John White, in his book *The Fight: A Practical Handbook for Christian Living*,[14] wrote these words:

> God does not change you by magic.
> No wand will be waved over your head
> so that your deepest problems vanish overnight.

---

[14] John White, *The Fight: A Practical Handbook for Christian Living* (Downers Grove, IL: InterVarsity Press, 1976), 112–113.

There may be a breakthrough,

sudden insights,

glorious experiences.

But the major work of transformation

will be slow and often deeply painful.

Yet the pain is immeasurably reduced by trust

and understanding.

Being meek means trusting Christ enough to turn the reins of our lives over to him, knowing full well that God wants to restore His image within us. The Creator desires to make us more ourselves than we have ever been before. Will we hand the reins over to God, knowing that growth is often painful and challenging? Do you—do I—trust God enough to be that kind of "meek"?

Blessed are the meek, for they will inherit the earth.

BEATITUDE 4

"BLESSED ARE THOSE WHO HUNGER AND THIRST FOR RIGHTEOUSNESS ..."

THE AUTHOR ROBERT Fulghum[15] tells a true story of a thirty-three-year-old truck driver by the name of Ken Walters, who was sitting in his lawn chair in his backyard one day while wishing he could fly. For as long as he could remember, Walters knew he wanted to fly, but he had never had the time, money, or opportunity to become a pilot. Hang gliding was out because there was no good place for gliding near his home. So he spent a lot of summer afternoons sitting in his

[15] Robert Fulghum, "All I Really Needed to Know I Learned in Kindergarten," reprinted in Esermons.com, February 25, 2003.

backyard in his ordinary, old, aluminum chair (the kind with the webbing and the rivets) that we all have in our backyards.

One day he decided to do something about his passion for flying. Ken hooked forty-five helium-filled surplus weather balloons to his chair, put a CB radio in his lap, tied a paper bag full of peanut butter and jelly sandwiches to his leg, and slung a BB gun over his shoulder to pop the balloons when he wanted to come down.

He lifted off in his lawn chair, expecting to climb a couple of hundred feet over his neighborhood. But instead, he shot up 11,000 feet, right through the approach corridor to the Los Angeles International Airport. It must have been quite a sight for a 747 to fly by a guy in a floating lounge chair, packing a BB gun and peanut butter sandwiches.

Somehow he made it down. When asked by the press why he did it, Ken answered, "Well, you can't just sit there." When asked if he was scared, he replied, "Yes. Wonderfully so." Ken Walters had a deep passion in his life, and he decided that day to go after that passion in a big way.

Let me ask this: If I were to give you an index card and a pencil and ask you to write down the main passion in your life, the thing in your life you have always hoped to do or accomplish but never had the chance, that one thing that you would both live for and be willing to die for, what would it be? What would your main passion be?

That's the message of the fourth Beatitude; God wants us to be passionate, to hunger, and to thirst for what Christ calls "righteousness." Now to understand what Jesus was getting at here, we need to remember that for most of us, the only time we hunger and thirst is right before we eat. But in Jesus's day, to hunger and thirst were needs you felt all the time. You see, the typical person in Palestine

- made just enough money each day to eke out an existence
- ate meat only once a week
- lived from meal to meal, hoping there would be food the next day
- had to beg for food or just starve if they got ill or injured and didn't work and their family wasn't wealthy

In Jesus's day, people knew all too well what it meant to go without food and water. So what Jesus was saying is that we are blessed (or on the right road with God) when we crave righteousness like a hungry person craves food and water.

But what is this "righteousness" that Christ wants us to crave? *Righteousness* is a fascinating word. Scholars tell us that initially it came from the Greek word *dikaios,* which means to "be instructed." You may remember that in Jesus's day, there were no public schools. Wealthy families would send kids off to a private academy. If they were highly affluent, the parents would hire a teacher to live with the family and teach their kids individually. When these young people grew up and lived according to what their teacher taught them, they were regarded to be righteous. This Beatitude is saying that God is our instructor and when we obey God's instructions for living, we are then "righteous."

Many today think of obedience to God's Word as restrictive, or as one person told me, obeying scripture is a "fun killer." In reality, it is just the opposite; it sets us free! I read an article about Jerry Rice, the NFL All-Pro wide receiver for the San Francisco 49ers who later played for the Oakland Raiders. Most consider him one of the finest football players ever to play the game. Yet he was almost unheard of when he got drafted. Many sportswriters asked, "Who is this guy?" or "Oh, what a mistake the 49ers have made with this no-name."

He showed up for his rookie training camp thinking he was in great physical shape but soon realized others on the team were fitter. Rice vowed that would never happen again. So in the off-season, when all the rest of the players were either resting or goofing off, Rice was in the gym. He developed an incredibly demanding workout regimen. Four hours a day, he ran wind sprints, lifted weights, stretched, and worked on his moves and pass routes. That was just the beginning. Then after that four-hour workout, he would either go running or play a round of golf.

Some would say that those hours in the gym or on the track sure must have cramped his style. His workout schedule indeed led him to a different lifestyle and off-season from the other players. But Jerry Rice didn't see it as something negative. Rice saw those hours of disciplined gym workouts, those thousands of miles he jogged, and those endless hours of running pass patterns setting him free to become the athlete he was created to be. The discipline gave him the freedom to keep playing at a high level when his peers had to retire, and it gave him the ability to set record after record on the field. What some described as a workout regimen that was confining, joyless, and endless drudgery, Rice relished. He understood his disciplined obedience to this off-season training plan was the key to his success.

It is no different with our spiritual lives. God has established a design for life, and we can either obey His plan or follow our own. Some will say that living according to God's design for life is "too confining," "joyless," or "old-fashioned." But it is through faithful obedience and seeking to abide in Christ that we will find the freedom to live with joyous fearlessness.

One of the saddest stories in the Bible is the life of Pontius Pilate, the Roman ruler who ultimately had Jesus crucified. Jesus was brought before Pilate three times, and each time, Pilate told the Jewish leaders that Jesus had done nothing wrong (Luke 23:14, 20, and 23) and did not deserve death. Even Pilate's wife sent a message telling him that she had suffered a frightful dream about Jesus, and she warned her husband to have nothing to do with Him (Matthew 27:19). But in the end, even the voice of Pilate's wife was drowned out by the angry demands of the Jewish leaders and crowd. It was easier for Pilate to give in to the pressures of a hostile crowd than heed the warning from a family member or do what he knew was right: free an innocent man from trumped-up charges. What should alarm us about this story is that we have done the same. No, we haven't had anyone crucified, but we have let others guide us into making decisions that we later regret. We have, at times, chosen to listen to the crowd instead of the voices of family, close friends, or God.

To hunger and thirst for righteousness means to have a craving to follow in the steps of Jesus. Doing so will lead us to live counterculturally. People seeking to follow Jesus will find ourselves turning away from cultural norms; Jesus people will spend money differently, live with different values, teach our children spiritual truths, and live with grace. We won't cheat on taxes or pad our expense accounts. We won't laugh at off-color jokes, repeat gossip, or have a critical spirit. We will speak up for those who can't speak for themselves. We will work faithfully at our careers, not just for a paycheck but to give honor and glory to Christ. You see, how we live depends on what we hunger and thirst for; let us hunger to be more like Jesus.

Blessed are those who hunger and thirst for
righteousness, for they will be filled.

※

BEATITUDE 5

"BLESSED ARE THE MERCIFUL ..."

I HAVE NEVER MUCH liked tests. That is probably because I never did very well on them. But some students flourish in academics. Some students are more clever than intelligent. One of my favorite test stories is of a college student who was bright and disciplined. He was taking an ornithology class (a class on birdlife). The professor was well-known for giving tough exams, so all the students studied hard and came to the classroom ready for the final exam. One gifted student studied extra hours for this test. On the day of the exam, the students took their seats. The professor uncovered a chart on the wall, revealing pictures of birds' feet. The professor said to his class, "Your final examination is simple. I want you to identify each bird by looking at their feet."

Well, the student was outraged. All the long hours of studying for this exam were a waste. He felt like no one could pass this exam! So he got up from his seat, went up to the professor's desk, and said, "Sir, this is ridiculous; you can't expect us to be able to do that."

"Why yes, I can. I am your teacher," said the professor. "This is your final exam."

"Well, what if I refuse?" said the student.

"If you refuse, then you will fail."

"Fine," said the student. "Fail me."

"OK," said the professor. "What is your name?"

The student pulled up his pants legs, pointed to his feet, and said, "You tell me."

I am sure that is an apocryphal story, but it does point to one truth: tests are never much fun. Yet sometimes tests are the only way to measure whether we are growing or not. The fifth Beatitude, "Blessed are the merciful," is kind of a test, a spiritual checkup to see how far we have grown in our walk with Christ. You see, the first four Beatitudes are about our relationship with Christ and cover much of the basics of the Christian faith. They focus on our brokenness and our need for a Savior.

But with this fifth Beatitude, the focus begins to shift. Where the first four Beatitudes focus on our need for God in our lives and how God meets those needs, the fifth Beatitude focuses on how believers should apply our faith in service to others. It is about putting our faith to work, and I have to tell you being merciful isn't easy. It requires spiritual maturity to be a merciful person. So as we begin, let me ask, "Would you describe yourself as a merciful person? Would those who know you best say you were merciful to others?"

When most of us think of the word *merciful,* we believe it means being nice to someone even though they may not deserve it. *Merciful* is a much richer word than that. The term *merciful* comes from the Hebrew word *chesed.* Now chesed is one of those words that can't be easily translated to English; there is just no English equivalent. Chesed means the ability to get right inside another person's skin until

- we can see things with their eyes
- think with their minds
- feel things with their feelings

It is the way God knows us. So Paul, in his letter to the Ephesians, describes how God cares for us. Paul writes in Ephesians 5:1–10,

> You were dead through the trespasses and sins in which you once lived, following the course of this world, following the ruler of the power of the air, the spirit that is now at work among those who are disobedient. All of us once lived among them in the passions of our flesh, following the desires of flesh and senses, and we were by nature children of wrath, like everyone

else. But God, who is rich in mercy, out of the great love with which he loved us even when we were dead through our trespasses, made us alive together with Christ—by grace you have been saved—and raised us up with him and seated us with him in the heavenly places in Christ Jesus, so that in the ages to come he might show the immeasurable riches of his grace in kindness toward us in Christ Jesus. For by grace you have been saved through faith, and this is not your own doing; it is the gift of God—not the result of works, so that no one may boast. For we are what he has made us, created in Christ Jesus for good works, which God prepared beforehand to be our way of life.

God didn't look down upon His creation and require that we get our act together before He would care for us. No, He fully understands what you and I go through every day. He knows our brokenness, struggles, joys, and pain, and in His mercy (chesed), He sent His son.

It is when we understand the depth of God's mercy (chesed) that Jesus bought us with His blood (Romans 3:21–26) that will move us from complacency to devotion. The mercy given to me by Christ, in turn, deepens my love for God and drives me to love others in that same way.

A few years ago, a study was done in Baltimore of two

hundred young, inner-city boys.[16] The project was to write a case history of each boy. To do that, the researchers looked at the boys' home life, education, social pressures, race, and so on. After each case history was written, the researcher would evaluate each boy's life situation and then write what they believed would be each boy's future. For virtually every boy, the researcher wrote, "He hasn't got a chance."

Twenty-five years later, another professor came across this earlier study and decided to do a follow-up study. What he found was astounding. With the exception of twenty boys who had died or could not be found, the study revealed that 176 of the remaining 180 boys had gone on to surprising success. Many became lawyers, doctors, and leading businessmen.

This finding was so surprising that the professor began to look for reasons these kids succeeded despite their apparent disadvantages. What they found was that they had all had one particular teacher who had influenced them. The teacher was still alive, so the professor set up an interview with her.

She was asked how she had influenced these boys who were destined for poverty and crime. How did these boys succeed when thousands of others didn't or couldn't? "It is really very simple," she responded. "I loved those boys."

Now, this teacher didn't love those kids with a mushy "I feel bad for those kids" kind of love. It is easy to feel bad for people. No, her love was a chesed love. She loved them enough to learn to see with their eyes, get into their skin, and feel what

---

[16] Eric Butterworth, *Chicken Soup for the Soul,* and reprinted in Preaching XI (July 1995), 41.

they felt. In spite of all they had going against them, she hung in there with them, encouraged them, and believed in them. She challenged them with high accountability for their actions and still loved them when they faltered. That's what chesed love, merciful love, looks like, and that's the way God has called us to love one another.

Mercy is loving someone enough to understand them yet caring for them enough not to leave them the way they are. Mercy (chesed) is love that transforms. We know that kind of mercy in Christ's love for us, which leads us to this important spiritual truth: *our capacity to show mercy to others is directly proportionate to our love for Christ.* The more we know and love Christ, the more mercy we will have for others!

Tony Campolo[17] tells a powerful story about how love transforms us. He writes of a time he was a counselor at a junior high camp. For most people, the hardest years of their lives are the middle school years, and being a camp counselor to that age group is particularly challenging. Quite often, a middle school kid's idea of a good time is picking on others. And at the camp that week, there was a young boy who was suffering from cerebral palsy. His name was Billy. He was an easy target, and others picked on him. When he walked across the campgrounds with his uncoordinated body, other campers would line up behind him, mimicking his uneven gate. One day, with great difficulty, Billy asked another kid for directions. Campolo was irate when he saw the other kids reply to Billy with twisted faces and halting speech. Then they laughed right to his face.

---

[17] http://www.theprodigalpig.com/?p=1019.

Campolo's anger peaked when the boys in Billy's cabin asked Billy to give the morning devotion. It was clear to Campolo that all those boys wanted to do was get Billy in front of the entire camp and humiliate him. But what Billy did surprised everyone. When he got to the microphone, Billy said just seven words in what seemed to be many minutes. Billy said, "Jesus loves me, and I love Jesus." But instead of jeers and laughter, Billy's message was met with absolute silence. In fact, some of the boys were crying. Soon a spiritual awakening broke out in that camp. Campolo reports that he would meet missionaries and preachers worldwide who would say, "Remember me? I was converted at that junior high camp."

Camp leaders had tried everything to get those middle school kids interested in Jesus. They even brought in baseball players whose batting averages had gone up when they had started praying. But God didn't use superstar athletes to reach those kids. God chose a kid with cerebral palsy to pierce the hearts of the other students. God often chooses the least likely. God chose Billy. Middle school boys who a moment ago were arrogant and mean-spirited were now humbled. The witness of this kid for Christ was so powerful that dozens of other campers gave their lives to Christ that week.

That junior high kid could have gotten to that microphone that morning and leveled the rest of those campers who had made fun of him. Billy wasn't dumb; he could have used that time to get even. But he had such a strong relationship with Christ that instead of getting revenge, Billy wanted the others to know the Lord he knew. That's what mercy looks like. It is not taking revenge or getting even with those who hurt us. It is letting our words and lives point to our Savior. It takes a mature faith for a believer to do that.

The last thing we need to understand about chesed is that it is a love that never gives up. Dr. Maxwell Matlz wrote a best-selling book called *Psycho-Cybernetics* and notes that a woman came to his office to talk about her husband one day. She told the doctor that her husband had been badly burned while attempting to save his parents from a burning home. Both were killed, and his face was terribly burned in the rescue attempt. The husband had given up on life and gone into hiding. He didn't want anyone to see him, not even his wife.

Dr. Matlz told her not to worry. "With great advances we've made in plastic surgery in recent years, I can restore his face." But she explained that he would not let anyone help him because he believed God had disfigured him to punish him for not saving his parents. Then she made a shocking request. "I want you to make my face burned-looking like his. If I can share in his pain, then maybe—he will let me back into his life. I love him so much; I want to be like him. And if that is what it takes, then that is what I want to do."

Of course, Dr. Matlz would not agree but persuaded her to let him try to talk to her husband. He went to the man's room and knocked on the door. "I know you are in there, and I know you can hear me, so I've come to tell you that my name is Dr. Maxwell Matlz. I am a plastic surgeon, and I want you to know I can restore your face."

There was no response.

Again, he called out, "Please come out and let me help restore your face."

No response.

Still talking through the door, Dr. Matlz told the man what his wife had asked him to do. "She wants me to make her face like yours in the hope that you will let her back into your life. That is how much she loves you. That's how much she wants to help you."

There was a brief silence, and then ever so slowly, the doorknob began to turn. Through the chesed of his wife, he came out of his hiding. Chesed from his wife gave him hope for a new life. That's what mercy (chesed) does. It changes us and those we love.

Blessed are the merciful, for they will receive mercy.

BEATITUDE 6

"BLESSED ARE THE PURE IN HEART ..."

SEVERAL YEARS AGO, the IRS received an unusual letter. It was clearly from someone with a guilty conscience. It went like this:

> Gentlemen: Enclosed, you will find a check for $150. I cheated on my income tax return last year and have not been able to sleep ever since.

That sounds admirable, doesn't it? The guy appears to have had a change of heart and is trying to square things with the IRS. But wait. The letter goes on:

If I still have trouble sleeping, I will send you the
rest. Sincerely …

We would all have to admit that this guy isn't the sharpest
pencil in the box. First, he confessed to the IRS that he cheated on
his taxes and still owes them money. Even more, I think we would
all agree that his motives were less than pure. Indeed, he was
moved to pay his past-due taxes not because it was the right thing
to do but because he was so guilt-ridden he couldn't sleep at night.

If we are honest, we would all have to admit that we at times
are like this guy. We too have mixed motives. Maybe our reasons
for doing the right thing aren't always as pure as we might profess.
We are all a collection of mixed motives and impure thoughts.

Yet Christ, in this sixth Beatitude, calls us to be pure in
heart. What does that mean? The word *pure* comes from the
Greek word *katharos,* and it has two meanings. The first meaning
of katharos is "to be cleansed." It is the word Greeks used for
washing dishes or washing their clothes, and it is where we get
the word *catharsis*[18] today.

We find this need for a catharsis throughout the Bible.
Maybe the most widely known appeal to God came from King
David. It happened after King David's sexual encounter with
Bathsheba and then having her husband murdered. David
was confronted by his best friend, Nathan. Ultimately, David
confessed his sin and turned to God for cleansing. In Psalm
51, David, full of guilt and regret, cried out to God. He prays,

---

[18] *Catharsis* is often used as a psychological term referring to being released
or cleansed from some feeling or belief that has someone bound.

Purge me with hyssop, and I shall be clean;

wash me, and I shall be whiter than snow.

Let me hear joy and gladness;

let the bones that you have crushed rejoice.

Hide your face from my sins, and blot out all my

iniquities. Create in me a clean heart, O God.

David was asking for God to do something only God could do. David wanted to be forgiven and cleansed. Our sins may be different from David's, but there will come many times in our lives where we too will need to ask for God's forgiveness and cleansing.

The second meaning of katharos is to be of one substance, unmixed or joined with anything else. Greek wine merchants sold wine in large jars or wineskins, and disreputable merchants would give samples of wine to their customers that would be all wine. The customers would buy the wine, thinking it was 100 percent wine, but when they got home, they opened the container to find that the wine had been watered down. This deception was such a common practice that in Jesus's day, wine merchants would advertise their wine as "katharos wine," which meant it was pure and not watered down.

So when Jesus told His disciples, "Blessed are the pure in heart," what He was saying is that we are on the right track with God when God cleanses our heart and our motives are not watered-down or mixed with other things. So how do we get a purified heart and life? Is it something we can do on our own? Can we achieve it by helping others or going to church more often? No, we don't purify ourselves. It is God who purifies us as we walk with Him.

I am sure some reading this book think that they have done something so grievous to God that they are beyond being forgiven, much less cleansed. Maybe it was one big sin that you have regretted most of your life. Or maybe your sins were just lots of little ones. And instead of seeing God as the One who loves us, we see God like this cruel judge just waiting to hammer us for the things we have done wrong.

Years ago, I read of an enterprising young man in Los Angeles who set up a rejection phone number for single women to use with men they disliked. The way it worked was if a woman met a man she didn't want to date and he asked for their phone number, the woman would give the man the phone number to the rejection phone line. Being curious about all this, I decided to give it a call on a Friday afternoon. The following is part of the message I heard:

> Maybe you are just not this person's type. This could mean that you are short, fat, ugly, dumb, annoying, arrogant, or just a general loser. Maybe you suffer from bad breath, body odor, or even both. Maybe you just give off that creepy, overbearing, psycho-stalker vibe. Maybe the idea of going out with you just seems as appealing as playing leapfrog with unicorns. Regardless of the reason, please take the hint.

That rejection line was so mean-spirited and painful to hear that I hung up before listening to the whole message. Some think that what was said on the rejection phone line is what God thinks of you or me. A loser. A reprobate. That God is dooming our lives to pain and strife and our souls are doomed for all time.

But that's not the way God feels about any of us. The prophet Ezekiel writes in 36:26 of a promise God makes to His followers.

> A new heart I will give you, and a new spirit I will
> put within you, and I will remove from your body
> the heart of stone and give you a heart of flesh.

Purity begins when we realize (like David) there is nothing we have done that is so bad that it is beyond the reach of God's love. God wants to wash us, make us clean again, and give us new hearts. Katharos—to be pure, to be washed—is a gift that God offers to one and all.

It is wonderful to be cleansed, be forgiven, and be given another chance in life! But being washed is not a one-time event. It is something I need almost daily. For that to happen, I need to stay Christ centered. The Bible calls that "abiding in Christ." Jesus says in John 15:4–5,

Abide in me as I abide in you. Just as the branch cannot bear fruit by itself unless it abides in the vine, neither can you unless you abide in me.

> I am the vine, you are the branches. Those who
> abide in me and I in them bear much fruit,
> because apart from me you can do nothing.

Jesus means we must stay connected. I heard of a[19] six-year-old girl who approached her father, who was working away one evening on his computer. He didn't notice that she was standing there but finally saw her and said, "Honey, is there something I can do for you?" She said, "Daddy, it is my bedtime. Mommy said if I came and stood beside you, you'd give me a hug and a kiss." "All right, you bet. Come here," he said. He gave her a big hug and a kiss and said, "Go off to bed now." And he went back to the computer, editing an essential report due the next day.

Ten minutes later, he noticed she was still there. He said, "Honey, I gave you a hug and a kiss. Is there something else you want?" She said, "Daddy, you gave me a hug and kiss, but you weren't in it."

That dad, no doubt well-intentioned, may have given her a hug and a kiss, but he wasn't in it. We can be guilty of the same. We can offer praise to someone but not be in it. We can preach a sermon and not be in it. We can come to worship God every Sunday and not be in it. We can use Christian lingo and play the part but not be in it. To be pure in heart means to have our hearts so grounded in the person of Jesus Christ that nothing else motivates us or guides us.

Josh McDowell[20] tells of the time he met an executive headhunter, which is someone who finds executives for large firms. This headhunter told McDowell that when he did executive interviews, he liked to disarm the candidates. He said,

---

[19] I believe this story came from a sermon from Tom Tewell, a PCUSA pastor.

[20] Josh McDowell's story is retold on Facebook by Many Waters Mission.

I would offer them a drink … take off my coat, undo my tie, put my feet on the desk, and talk about baseball, football, family, whatever makes them feel relaxed. Then, when I think I have them relaxed, I lean over, look them square in the eye, and say, "What's your purpose in life?" It's amazing how top executives fall apart at that question.

He then told McDowell of an interview he recently had where the exec was disarmed and relaxed; his feet were up on the desk and talking football. Then he leaned over and said, "What's your purpose in life, Bob?" And without blinking an eye, Bob said, "To go to heaven and take as many people with me as I can." The headhunter went on. "For the first time in my life, I was speechless."

Now you and I might not express our faith just like Bob, but we all have to agree that he was focused and grounded in his faith. He was Christ centered; he was abiding in Jesus. That's what a pure heart looks like. It is unmixed, uncompromised, and of one substance, Jesus Christ.

Blessed are the pure in heart, for they will see God.

BEATITUDE 7

"Blessed are the Peacemakers ..."

Many traditional churches take a moment each Sunday morning when members in the pews are asked to greet those sitting around them. Some churches call this the "passing of the peace." A church in the Pacific Northwest[21] had been doing this for years. Each Sunday, members of the congregation would hug, greet each other, and say, "Peace be with you." Newcomers were equally welcomed with a kind word or maybe a hug. Nobody thought much about the weekly ritual until the pastor received a letter from a man who had recently joined the congregation. The new member

---

[21] William G. Carter, *Water Won't Quench the Fire,* CSS Publishing Company.

was a promising young lawyer from a prestigious downtown law firm. He drafted a brief but pointed letter on his firm's letterhead, which read,

> I am writing to complain about the congregational ritual known as "passing the peace." I disagree with it, both personally and professionally, and I am prepared to take legal action to cause this practice to cease.

The pastor phoned the lawyer about the letter and asked why he was so disturbed by the custom. The lawyer said, "The passing of the peace is an invasion of my privacy." The minister had a winsome reply. He said, "Like it or not, when you joined the church, you gave up some of your privacy, for we believe in a risen Lord who will never leave us alone." Then he added, "You never know when Jesus Christ will intrude on us with a word of peace." How true.

Jesus, the Prince of Peace, was sending a clear message in this Beatitude about the importance of peace. Peace is something we, as humans, have struggled with since time began.

According to one writer,[22]

- in all of recorded history, there has been peace in the world only 8 percent of the time
- in the last 3,600 years, only 292 of those years have been peaceful

---

[22] Paul Lee Tan, *Encyclopedia of 7,700 Illustrations* (Hong Kong: Nordica International 1979), 1571.

- in that time, approximately 8,000 treaties were made, and almost all were violated
- there have been 14,531 wars (both large and small)

According to the *Canadian Army Journal,* if you take the cost of all those wars and convert it into gold, you could build a golden road around the circumference of the earth that was 97.2 miles wide and thirty-three feet thick.

Peace among nations has always been a challenge. And there is another kind of peace that our souls long for—peace within our hearts. We yearn for peace, search for it, and drug ourselves to feel it (even if it is artificial), and it remains elusive for most. But this is nothing new. In the 1960s, people searched for peace with sex, drugs, and alcohol. That was a disaster. In the seventies, people searched for peace through individualism; it was the me decade, which equally was a failure. Selfishness always fails. In the eighties and nineties, people searched for peace through materialism. That got people in debt and left them unsatisfied. And the last thirty years? Well, Generation X, millennials, and Generation Z have all had their turn, but it is safe to say that few know peace.

Where does that peace we long for really come from? How do we find peace and become the peacemakers that Christ calls us to be? Scripture teaches that our source of peace that we all want in our life does not come from something but from someone. The apostle Paul wrote:

(Eph. 2:14a) "For He [Christ] is our peace;" and (Eph. 2:17) "So He [Christ] came and proclaimed peace to you who were far off and peace to those who were near" Christ is the source of our peace. It is when we give Him our hearts, our lives, our careers, and even those we love. It is when we empty ourselves and follow Him that we find the peace only He can give.

Joan Webb wrote in her book *Meditations for Christians Who Try to Be Perfect* these words:

> Years ago, after I asked God to fill my cup, it seemed, instead, that he ate my lunch. As I saw my dreams fade away, I worked hard to hold on and eventually burned out. I wondered where God was and why he let it happen. Now, as I reflect back, I wonder if he could not fill my cup because I already had it full with my personal agenda. I wanted to accomplish great things for God, but I had my own ideas. Perhaps he was waiting for me to empty the unusable contents so he could pour in his plan.

Christmas has always been a wondrous time with my family, especially when our sons were young. Being a Presbyterian minister, we had very few relaxing holiday seasons. After all, the word *holiday* came from the words *holy days,* the busiest time of year for clergy.

One Christmas morning, I was caffeine fueled; my family and I were opening presents. Our den looked like a bomb had gone off; wrapping paper, empty gift boxes, visiting grandparents, two kids, and a ninety-pound Labrador made it all a joyous mess. I looked at my six-year-old with opened gift boxes and wrapping paper almost covering him up and his arms loaded with new toys. He turned to me and said, "Is this all?"

He didn't say it in a selfish way. He just wanted to know if there were more gifts to open. I thought, *I'm glad there are no more presents; there is no room in his arms, bedroom, or toybox for one more.* Then it hit me; we are all like my six-year-old on Christmas morning. Our lives are overflowing with stuff (some good, some not so good) yet wanting more. And the truth is there is much more. Jesus has more for us than we could ever imagine, but like my son, there is often no room in our lives. Someone said, "Americans are the only people in the world whose cups overflow, and instead of being thankful, we complain about the size of our cups."

When we get to heaven, I wonder if Jesus will take us into a colossal room to show us all the things He wanted to shower us with if we had only made room. Wonderful gifts, peace, missional hearts, kindness, a sturdy faith, purpose, and so much more. Yet our lives were too full, too busy, to receive or even appreciate anything else. The spiritual lesson is this: emptying is a prerequisite to filling. Our overflowing, busy lives yield stress and anxiety. God's portion produces security and peace.

PEACEMAKERS: LEARN FORGIVENESS

Peace, for most people, begins when we learn to forgive. Jesus commands us to forgive. It is not a suggestion; if you follow Jesus, this is nonnegotiable. Yet for many believers, anger, resentment, and holding grudges have taken root in our hearts. I am continually amazed how many people hold on to old wounds and hard feelings for years, and like a spiritual cancer, it just eats us up inside.

Corrie ten Boom[23] was a woman who, during WWII, was a prisoner in the German extermination camp called Ravensbruck. She was arrested for helping Jews escape evil Nazi occupation. She was a devout Christian, and her faith was instrumental in her survival. Faith always is. The conditions within Ravensbruck were horrific, and she knew she might be killed at any moment. Due to a clerical error, she was released just five days before the other women her age were killed.

Two years after the war ended, she was in Munich, Germany, speaking to a group about forgiveness. As she was talking, she saw in the crowd a man who had been one of the prison guards where she was a prisoner. He had taken part in many of the atrocities. But now she watched as the man worked his way through the crowd. He stood in front of her and thrust out his hand to shake hers. He said, "A fine message. Fraulein! How good it is to know that, as you say, all our sins are at the bottom of the sea!"

And here I will pick up the story in Corrie ten Boom's own words.

And I, who had spoken so glibly of forgiveness, fumbled in my pocketbook rather than take that hand. He would not remember me, of

---

[23] https://doctorchris.org/corrie-ten-boom-confronts-the-nazi-guard/. At this site, you can even hear her tell this story in a recording.

course—how could he remember one prisoner among those thousands of women? But I remembered him and the leather crop swinging from his belt. I was face-to-face with one of my captors, and my blood seemed to freeze.

"You mentioned Ravensbruck in your talk," he was saying. "I was a guard there." No, he did not remember me. "But since that time," he went on, "I have become a Christian. I know that God has forgiven me for the cruel things I did there, but I would like to hear from your lips as well. "Fraulein,"—again his hand came out—"will you forgive me?"

It could not have been many seconds that he stood there—handheld out—but to me, it seemed hours as I wrestled with the most difficult thing I had ever had to do ... I stood there with the coldness clutching my heart. But forgiveness is not an emotion—I knew that too. Forgiveness is an act of the will, and the will can function regardless of the temperatures of the heart. "Jesus, help me!" I prayed silently. "I can lift my hand. I can do that much. You supply the feeling." And so woodenly, mechanically, I thrust my hand into the one stretched out to me. As I did, an incredible thing took place. The current started in my shoulder, raced down my arm, sprang into our joined hands. And then this healing warmth seemed to flood my whole being, bringing tears to my eyes. "I forgive you, brother," I cried. "With all my heart." For a long moment, we grasped each other's hands, the former guard and the former prisoner. I had never known God's love so intensely as I did then. But even so, I realized it was not my love. I had tried and did not have the power. It was the power of the Holy Spirit (Romans 5:5) that had poured God's love into my heart.

That was a holy moment. The Holy Spirit gave Corrie ten Boom the power to do what she could not do alone. In forgiving the guard, she experienced God more profoundly than ever before. The reward for forgiving someone is, of course, removing an old grudge (a spiritual blockage to our growth), but the better reward is experiencing more of God.

PEACEMAKING IS A VERB

Peacemaking begins when we find within us a peace that only Jesus Christ can give. But it is more than that. As we receive peace from our Savior, we are to serve those who God puts in our path. If Jesus is directing your steps and mine, He is also directing the steps of those around us. So as you go where the Lord takes you, He will set up divine appointments with those in need. Meeting those needs is peacemaking.

I want to tell you about the time I met Moses. After

Thanksgiving in 2001, I was at my church with a couple of other church members, decorating the exterior for Christmas. We had a great time hanging wreaths and putting some twinkling white lights in bushes around the historic sanctuary.

With most offices closed downtown on weekends, it was not uncommon for the homeless to gather around churches. Sometimes they would crash wedding receptions or even funerals to get out of the cold and grab some catered food.

This Saturday morning was no different. We had a few people come by to use the bathroom or ask for money. Then as we were wrapping up our work, we noticed a rather well-dressed person who was shaved and groomed except for one thing that was hard to miss. He wasn't wearing any shoes. He had socks on but no shoes. He approached us shyly, almost acting embarrassed. As he got closer, he didn't say anything; he just stood there. So I asked if we could help him in some way. No response. I asked him if his feet were cold. No answer. I asked him his name. He finally responded, "Moses." I told him that was a pretty famous name and asked if he had a last name. "No, just Moses," he said.

I could tell this guy (maybe in his late twenties) had some mental challenges. So I asked him if he had a place to stay and if he was hungry. Again, no response. Finally, I asked if he needed shoes. He said nothing. I was wearing some old basketball shoes (so this was no colossal sacrifice), took them off, and offered them to him, expecting him not to take them. But to my surprise, he sat down on the curb and put them on. Then he stood up and, not saying a word, just walked away. My coworker laughed and said, "Well, I didn't think I would meet Moses this morning."

I never thought we would ever see Moses again, but that's not the end of the story. Twenty-four hours later, he showed up early before the worship service. He said his name was Moses again. I asked him if he wanted some coffee. He nodded. So I grabbed a cup of coffee for him. After he took a sip, he acted like he wanted to give me something. I said, "Moses, there is no charge." But this seemed to aggravate him. He kept extending his arm like he wanted to pay for the coffee, and a colleague close by said, "I think he wants to tip you." So I held out my hand, and he placed an imaginary coin in my hand and then smiled, which was the first emotion we had seen him show. This scenario went on each Sunday for about a month. In all that time, Moses would not speak to anyone other than to share his name. And he liked to give an imaginary tip to anyone who paid attention to him or helped him in some way.

The Sunday before Christmas Eve, Moses was at church again earlier than the rest of God's people. I saw him come in but didn't see him leave. After the worship service, I asked one of our church leaders if he had seen Moses that morning. He said, "Yes, Moses came to church at his regular time, but soon afterward, an older man came into the fellowship hall. He took Moses by the hand and led him toward the exit doors. Moses seemed to be glad to go with him. So I asked the older man if we could help him in some way. He said he was the young man's father. They had been searching for him. With sad eyes, the father said, 'Tell the church I am grateful for the way you treated my son.'"

I wish I could have met that dad. But I was so proud to be in a church that would love and give care to a lost soul like Moses. No one made fun of him or asked me to tell him to leave. We made room for a guy who called himself Moses until his father could find him. Sometimes a church will be a university—a place for learning—sometimes it will be a hospital—for those who are broken—and sometimes a church should be an oasis for people lost in life—like Moses. That's what peacemaking looked like that Advent season at our church. Moses was a blessing to us.

That's peacemaking. We don't have to go looking for opportunities to make peace. Jesus is choreographing it all for us. We just need to allow Jesus to guide our steps; He will bring the opportunity to us.

> Blessed are the peacemakers, for they
> shall be called children of God.

BEATITUDE 8

"BLESSED ARE THOSE WHO HAVE BEEN PERSECUTED ..."

NOT TOO LONG ago, I was visiting someone in the hospital who had just had a baby. I got in the elevator to go to the maternity floor when a new dad and his mother or mother-in-law (I couldn't tell which) got on the elevator with me. It was evident that he was a new dad because he had an enormous smile on his face, his clothes were a wrinkled mess, and he looked like he hadn't slept in days.

It was amazing that the three of us fit in this elevator because this father had a huge, stuffed, black bear in one arm and the other arm held a tiny tricycle and a football helmet. His mom (or mother-in-law) carried all the luggage. As the elevator ascended from floor to floor, that very kind woman kept saying, "I don't know why you are bringing all this stuff to the room. He is only a day old; he isn't even going to know what all this is." Her words had no impact on the new dad. He was so proud of his new son that he wanted to make sure he got a good start in life.

That mom (or mother-in-law) was right. It would be years before that newborn would know what all that stuff was. Growing up takes time. It is a process that happens over months, years, and decades. It is the same with our spiritual lives. When we begin our faith journey, we are not instantly spiritually mature. That takes time. However, if we never mature, that is an alarming signal that something is wrong. We should be more Christlike five years from now than we are today. And we should be more Christlike today than we were five years ago. Sadly, that is usually not the case.

Many Christians begin their walk with Christ in high school or college. For a while, they would attend a Bible study or church. But over time, that fades away. Even though Christ remains a part of their life, His role changes from Lord to advisor. For some, He becomes a silent partner. It doesn't have to be that way.

And one of the chief ways of gauging our spiritual maturity is by looking at our capacity to love others. We have said that it is easy to love those who love you back. It is harder to love spiritual porcupines, those we know who are friendly at first and become pricklier as we grow closer to them. Loving those we don't know (or those we may never meet) may be the third level of love. But maybe the most challenging is loving those who persecute us. Only those who have logged many miles with Jesus will be able to love those who attack, mock, or mistreat us in some way for our faith. That kind of love is at the heart of the last Beatitude.

Christ is telling His followers (then and today) that following Him might be very costly. That is because following Christ means we should live differently from the rest of the world. We will have different values. We will spend our time seeking to fulfill God's value systems and not the world's. As Easter people, we will raise our kids with different priorities from secular parents. Our kids won't watch the same kind of movies or TV as others their age. Our vocabulary will be distinctly gracious, and our sense of humor will be much different. In short, how we live as Jesus followers will set us apart from the non-Christian world. That's what Paul means when he says that Christians are to be in the world but not of the world.

Leith Anderson, one of this generation's best preachers, tells the story[24] of when he was a young man just entering the ministry as an assistant. He was on the staff of a large church, he loved his boss and the church, and the church loved him. He was growing in his faith and prospering in his ministry.

Then he discovered the church had some financial problems, and to his shock, the finance committee decided the best way to handle the shortage was to fire Leith. Even though years passed, he remembers this as one of the worse moments

[24] Leith Anderson, *Leadership That Works* (Bloomington, MN: Bethany House 1999) 169–170.

of his life. He kept asking, "God, how can these people do this to me?"

To make matters even worse, the very next day, a deacon called him and said, "Hey, Leith, the senior minister has been called out of town. We can't find anyone else to preach, and anyway, since you are still on staff till the end of the month, we knew we could get you for free." Leith thought, *Boy, this is my chance. I am going to let these people know how I feel.* But something inside said, "Oh no, you don't. You love those people. You teach the scriptures just like always." That is precisely what Leith did.

Two months later, the senior minister (his old boss) was called to another church. A search for a new senior minister began, and then the church leadership chose Leith to be their pastor. He served there for ten great years.

That Sunday so long ago, Leith could have chosen vengeance, or he could choose a different path—one that was loving and gracious. He chose love, and God honors that.

Sometimes we can see how God redeems someone who has been wronged or persecuted. Those are extraordinary times, but it doesn't always work out like that. Often we will follow Jesus and be mistreated. In those moments, we are to love Jesus even though we may never see a happy ending.

Sarah Shin's timely and insightful book *Beyond Colorblind*[25] recalls a story of a college student named Brent. He was a young Black man who had endured many racist experiences growing up. But while in college, he got involved with a multiethnic

---

[25] Sarah Shin, *Beyond Colorblind*, Intervarsity Press, Downers Grove, IL, 2017, 83–84.

Christian community that helped him forgive those who had mistreated him.

One day, Brent, the school's track team captain, was at practice when a truck full of White men drove up and yelled threats at Brent. They went up and down the practice field, yelling at him and threatening his life. One of them even stuck his head out the truck's window and called to Brent by name.

Afterward, Brent and his friends were angry at the verbal threats and gathered to pray. The college administration heard about the racist assailment and told Brent, "We will not tolerate people like that at our school. We will expel them and prosecute them. We don't need those people on our campus."

But Brent's remarkable response shocked them all. He said, "Those people? Don't you get it? You're one of *those* people. I'm one of *those* people. Don't act like they're some outside force. Because those guys were taught and encouraged to hate in their schools, churches, and maybe even on this campus. How can you say you want to educate when you don't want to embrace?" He went on. "If there should be a punishment, it should be forcing them to sit down with me over dinner to get to know me for the next several weeks." Brent knew the name of at least one of those White men in the truck but would not release it. A CNN reporter asked Brent why he would defend those who committed such a vile assault. He replied, "Because I love him. And you protect those you love."

Through Brent's faith, his community of believers, and the power of the Spirit, he spoke words that were well beyond what most of us would have said. He knew the power of loving those who hate or persecute. Brent had learned and put into practice what Jesus taught His disciples: love always wins. Maybe not immediately, but ultimately love wins. Jesus will have the last word, so we are free to love courageously.

It is one thing to love someone who has wronged us, but how do we love whole communities that persecute us for our faith? Sociologists and church historians report that we have entered a post-Christian age in our country, meaning that Christian influences will continue to diminish in our culture. As our culture is increasingly rejecting values that Christ taught, those who follow Christ will likewise find themselves at odds with the currents of our culture.

Already, believers worldwide have it far more challenging to live faithful lives than those of us in America. Did you know the following?[26]

- A Christian research firm affiliated with Gordon-Conwell Center for the Study of Global Christianity in Massachusetts estimates over 900,000 Christians were martyred from 2007 to 2017.
- That is 90,000 martyred Christians per year.
- One Christian, somewhere in the world, is killed for their faith every six minutes.
- Rev. Dr. Juhana Pohjola, diocesan dean and bishop-elect of the Evangelical Lutheran Mission Diocese of Finland (ELMDF), was charged by Finland's prosecutor

---

[26] https://www.christianpost.com/news/over-900000-christians-martyred-for-their-faith-in-last-10-years-report-173045/.

general with incitement against a group of people.[27] The charges stem from a 2004 booklet that purports the historic Christian teaching on human sexuality.

While Christians in America are not being arrested or martyred for following Jesus at this time, storm clouds of persecution are gathering on the horizon. Biblical principles on marriage, abortion, and even personal liberties will increasingly be challenged by a secular society. We must stay true to Christ no matter the cost.

The first time I experienced the high cost of following Jesus came when I was in college. While attending the University of South Florida in Tampa, I was a Young Life volunteer leader and later was invited to be a part-time college staff person. In my dorm, I met many other students with different faith traditions. One such student was Nick (not his real name). Nick was from south Florida, had a fancy wardrobe, wore a *chai* (necklace with Hebrew letters that meant "life"), and drove a brand-new car. We were as different as night and day but became friends.

I cannot imagine having a better college experience. About thirty college students were volunteering with Young Life, including Virginia, who would later become my wife. These thirty students had fun leading the ministry together and just being together as brothers and sisters in Christ. Some got apartments together; others stayed in the dorms. It would not

---

[27] https://www.theaquilareport.com/finnish-bishop-elect-charged-over-historic-christian-teachings-on-human-sexuality/.

be unusual for all of us to gather at someone's apartment for a meal or to watch a movie. It was a true Christian community.

Each week, about six to eight of us gathered in my dorm room to pray together and go over our plans for the Young Life club meeting that would be happening later that night. After a few weeks, I noticed that Nick, my friend with another faith, stayed in the dorm room and quietly listened to us as we planned, laughed, practiced songs, and closed by praying together. After about a month, Nick told me that this leadership team treated each other very differently from how he and his friends treated each other. Nick said that there was respect and a noticeable lack of sarcasm. He asked me why we laughed so much. Nick found it amazing that college students would spend so much time working with high school students and not get paid.

I asked him if he would like to join us one week and attend the Young Life club we were leading. He said he needed to think about that. Honestly, I can't remember whether he ever went with us to a club meeting or not. But what was more important was our conversations continued.

The conversations began in October. In the following months, we discussed topics like the following:

- Who was Jesus?
- Do Christians hate Jews?
- How does the Old Testament fit together with the New Testament?
- Did I believe the world was getting more or less sinful?

I was woefully unprepared for most of these discussions. All I knew to do was share what I knew, confess what I didn't, and love Nick like the brother he was.

It was mid-December, and the semester was coming to a close. Amid finals week, Nick and I had a late-night conversation. He wanted to know more about Jesus, and after more than an hour of talking, I dropped the hammer. I asked, "Nick, do you want to follow Jesus?" He asked me what that meant, and I told him it meant surrendering your life to the Life Giver Jesus Christ. I mentioned that Jesus came to give us an abundant life (John 10:10) and that Jesus had a plan for his life and career—designed just for him. He said he needed to think about it. We both got busy after that night, finishing up final exams, and I was helping to lead a Young Life snow ski trip over the Christmas break, so life was gloriously busy.

After Christmas break, I ran into Nick again on campus. Surprisingly, he didn't seem too happy to see me. I wondered if I had offended him somehow. Too pushy maybe? Life got busy again, so days went by. Then one night, Nick came by and wanted to talk. I asked him if I had offended him in some way. He said no, but he had been thinking about this "Jesus thing." He told me he had thought about it over the winter break and finally decided to talk to his parents about it. Nick said that his parents were upset at the thought of him becoming a Christian. They told him that if he converted, they would have a funeral service for him, he would no longer be welcomed at family events, and he would be removed from their will. Whoa. I had no idea he would have to pay such a huge price for following

Jesus. We both were silent for a long time. I didn't know what to say. I had no words.

Inside, I wanted him to say that he would follow Jesus, but another part of me understood his hesitation. Was I disappointed? Yes, of course. I would have loved to have Nick as a brother in Christ. But deep down, I wondered if I had been in Nick's shoes, would I have done the same? I like to think I would have given up millions of dollars and my family to serve the King of Kings. I was just grateful that I didn't have to make that choice. That was the first time I had ever witnessed the price that some must pay to follow Jesus. I suspect that future generations will experience persecution we would never imagine.

A few years ago, I was privileged to have a meal with a missionary from India named Matthew (not his real name to protect his identity). At dinner, someone asked him how they started their ministry in India. He said they had spent many years reaching communities, and people were making professions of faith, but there were few churches so many of these new believers never had a faith community that would help them grow.

So they decided to start a church, and after almost a year's work, they had seventeen people who were sold out to Christ. He said that when someone wanted to become a believer, they were asked these questions:

- "Have you invited Jesus Christ into your life?"
- "Are you willing to die for Jesus?"
- "Are you willing to never forsake or denounce Jesus even if you are tortured or killed?"

Of the seventeen people who said that they were willing to die if necessary for Christ, two were Muslim women. Matthew said that within a few weeks of their conversion, both women just disappeared. Matthew said they were killed for their faith. That didn't stop the other fifteen believers. They continued working and serving, and today there are a couple of hundred small churches that have been started.

As American culture moves further away from our Judeo-Christian values, the price to follow Christ will escalate. As the costs go up, so must our love. That can only happen as we become more and more like Jesus and we let the love of our Lord pass through us to the world around us.

Blessed are those who have been persecuted for the sake of righteousness, for theirs is the kingdom of heaven. Rejoice and be glad, for your reward is great in heaven, for in the same way they persecuted the prophets who were before you.

CONCLUSION

Everyone has within them the capacity to love. It is a gift from God, who is love Himself. This love has the power to change the hearts and lives of all who encounter it. For example, there is an insightful story of a guy named Pete,[28] who after two years of marriage no longer saw his wife as interesting, fun, or attractive. In his mind, she had let herself go and didn't keep the house the way he wanted, and he saw her as being overbearing. He not only wanted to divorce his wife but also wanted to hurt her as she had disappointed him. So he contacted this wise, old divorce attorney for counsel. The attorney told him, "Pete, if you really want to get even with your wife, start treating her like a queen! Do everything in your power to serve her and please her. Take her out every once in a while, even take her to church. Just try to make her feel special. Then after a couple of

---

[28] Author unknown; similar story published at https://karenbjae.blogspot.com/. Another very similar version of the story was published by J. Allen Peterson at http://www.sermonillustrations.com/a-z/l/love.htm.

months of this royal treatment, pack your bags and leave. That way, you will disappoint her as much as she disappointed you."

Pete thought this was a great idea. So on the way home, he picked up a dozen roses. After dinner, he helped her with the dishes. Pete then started bringing her breakfast in bed and complimented her on her clothes, cooking, and housekeeping. He even planned for some weekend getaways, and they started going to church.

A few months later, the attorney just happened to run into Pete at the mall and asked him how things were going and if he wanted to proceed with the divorce. Pete said, "No way! These have been the best months of our marriage. She is a changed woman. My wife is the best wife any man could want." And the wise old attorney just smiled.

The truth is they both had changed. Love does that. When Pete's wife felt loved and appreciated, she loved Pete more and more. The more she loved Pete, the more he wanted to serve and please her. Love changes people, changes marriages, and changes communities. Now imagine if your love for your family, friends, and neighbors could be increased not by just a little but multiplied many times over. Imagine being able to love others the way Jesus loves you. Jesus wants to give that gift to you.

It begins when we realize we are spiritually poor and need a Savior (Beatitude 1: "Poor in Spirit"). Then we continue to grow when we mourn over our past sins and turn to God (Beatitude 2: "Mourn"). Then when we surrender to Jesus, not in just a part of our lives but when we put our lives under his care (Beatitude 3: "Meek"), the adventure of faith begins to pick up momentum. Next we realized that we have developed a craving to please the Lord like a starving person seeks food (Beatitude 4: "Hunger and Thirst for Righteousness"); that's when our life begins to go in a new faithful direction. Soon we realize the things that used to send us into fits of anger or frustration just don't seem to bother us anymore (Beatitude 5: "Merciful") and we are kinder to people, even to those who don't deserve it. The next step (Beatitude 6: "A Pure Heart") is when the world's influences diminish and the Spirit's guidance becomes more and more the primary rudder in our life. Then one Sunday, you will be in church and the preacher will be a missionary from someplace on the other side of the planet. Hearing him tell of the suffering and persecution that others endure moves you to get personally involved, and you realize you have become a peacemaker (Beatitude 7). Finally, at your workplace, your boss wants you to change some reports before she presents them to the board. You know what she is asking you to do is deceiving the board, so you politely decline by saying that you checked the numbers and you know them to be correct. From that point on, you are relegated to the boss's B team. When the next round of pay increases are announced, you are not on the list. You are hurt and disappointed, but you know that the Lord smiled at your decision to stay faithful (Beatitude 8: "Persecuted"). Instead of hating your boss, you feel sorry for her and add her to your prayer list.

In my walk of faith, this spiritual growth cycle has happened more times than I can count. And each time, the Lord shows me something in my life that He wants to redeem. When I become aware of this need in my life, the cycle begins over again. I find myself more and more like Jesus. I see the world a little more like Jesus sees it. I pass a public school and begin to pray for those teachers and students. I see homeless people, and my heart breaks as I know this is someone's mother/father or son/daughter. When I see racial injustice, I am not incited to go to the streets with hate but to allow the Lord to bring into my life people I am to love the way Jesus loves me.

Following Jesus is a great adventure. An unknown author[29] described what it was like surrendering to Christ. He wrote this:

> At first, I saw God as my observer, my judge, keeping track of the things I did wrong, so as to know whether I merited heaven or hell when I die. He was out there, sort of like a president. I recognized His picture, but I didn't really know him. But later on, when I met Christ, it seemed as though life were rather like a bike ride, but it was a tandem bike, and I noticed that Christ was in the back helping me pedal.

> I don't know just when it was that He suggested we change places, but life has not been the same since. When I had control, I knew the way. It was rather boring and predictable. It was the shortest distance between two points.

---

[29] https://www.cybersalt.org/illustrations/the-road-of-life, "The Road of Life," author unknown.

But when He took the lead, He knew delightful long cuts up mountains and through rocky places at break-neck speeds; it was all I could do to hang on! Even though it looked like madness, He said, "Pedal!" I worried and was anxious and asked, "Where are you taking me?" He laughed and didn't answer, and I started to learn to trust.

I forgot my boring life and entered the adventure. And when I'd say, "I'm scared!" He'd lean back and touch my hand. He took me to people with gifts that I needed, gifts of healing, acceptance, and joy. They gave me gifts to take on my journey, my Lord's and mine. And we were off again. He said, "Give the gifts away; they're extra baggage, too much weight." So I did, to the people we met, and I found that in giving I received, and still our burden was light.

I did not trust Him, at first, in control of my life, I thought He'd wreck it, but He knows bike secrets, knows how to make it bend to make sharp corners, knows how to jump to clear high rocks, knows how to fly to shorten scary passages. And I am learning to be quiet and pedal in the strangest places, and beginning to enjoy the view, and the cool breeze on my face, with my delightful constant companion, JESUS

CHRIST. And when I'm sure I just can't do it anymore, He just smiles and says ... "Pedal."

That's what it looks like to follow Jesus. And the longer we follow, the more we become like Him. That includes *loving like Jesus.*

The Beatitudes

Matthew 5:1–11

When Jesus saw the crowds, he went up the mountain; and after he sat down, his disciples came to him. Then he began to speak, and taught them, saying:
Blessed are the poor in spirit, for theirs is the kingdom of heaven.
(You are on the right path when you recognize that you are a sinner in need of a Savior and that Savior is Jesus.)

Blessed are those who mourn, for they will be comforted.
(Kneel before your Maker and share your broken heart,
and He will give you His strength, the strength to take just one more step.)

Blessed are the meek, for they will inherit the earth.
(Meek people have strength under God's control.)

Blessed are those who hunger and thirst for righteousness, for they will be filled.

(You are on the right track with God when you strive to live holy lives.)

Blessed are the merciful, for they will receive mercy.

(You are abiding with Christ when you accept His transforming loving-kindness

and give that same loving-kindness to others.)

Blessed are the pure in heart, for they will see God.

(You are on the right road with God when you have experienced a cleansed heart.)

Blessed are the peacemakers, for they shall be called children of God.

(You make Jesus smile when you help others find shalom.)

Blessed are those who have been persecuted for the sake of righteousness, for theirs is the kingdom of heaven. Rejoice and be glad, for your reward is great in heaven, for in the same way they persecuted the prophets who were before you.

(Following Jesus may bring on persecution, if so, keep your eyes on Jesus and know that God will have the last word.)

Made in the USA
Las Vegas, NV
28 February 2023